BUILDING OXFORD'S HERITAGE

SYMM & COMPANY from 1815

BUILDING OXFORD'S HERITAGE

SYMM & COMPANY from 1815

BRIAN R. LAW

Foreword by
Sir Howard Colvin

With an introduction by
David Sturdy

Following a suggestion by John Besley, Director and Company Secretary 1972-1991, historian Anne Sharpe commenced research for this history of Symm in 1991 based on a sketchy sheet of handed-down information. The more Anne researched, the more she uncovered the wealth of the firm's fascinating and perhaps unique history since the birth of the founder Daniel Evans around 1769. Malcolm Axtell, great-grandson of Joshua Symm's partner, Thomas Axtell, became the driving force behind the production of this book and personally researched early archive photographs, engravings, drawings and original documents.

Author Brian R. Law's book is a tribute to those talented Symm craftsmen and staff members whose skills and abilities have helped to create so much of the University of Oxford's historic building heritage over almost two centuries.

First published in 1998 by
Prelude Promotion
Avoca, Brookhampton
Stadhampton
Oxford   OX44 7XR
Tel: +44 (0) 1865 891761

Symm Group incorporates: Symm and Company Ltd., Axtell Perry Symm Masonry Ltd. and Sharp and Howse Ltd.

British Library Cataloguing in Publication Data
Law, Brian R.
        Building Oxford's Heritage

ISBN 0 9532873 0 0 Hardback

Designed by Yvonne Macken
Prelude Promotion, Oxford

Printed in Hong Kong through Worldprint

Frontispiece: Oxford: City of Dreaming Spires

CONTENTS

FOREWORD
by Sir Howard Colvin   7

INTRODUCTION: Builders, Architects and Clients
by David Sturdy   9

Map of Oxford 1817   18

Map of Oxford 1994   19

I   THE OXFORD BUILDING TRADE   21

II   THE FOUNDATIONS: 1815-1846   29
      Daniel Evans, Founder

III   GOTHIC REVIVAL: 1846-1887   43
      Joshua Robinson Symm

IV   A NEW PARTNERSHIP   73
      Symm and Company: 1887-1926

V   TO THE PRESENT DAY   91
      Symm and Company: 1926-1998

VI   THE FUTURE FOR SYMM   115

      Appendix: Chronological List of Buildings by SYMM   126

      Note on the value of money   132

      Acknowledgements   132

      Picture Acknowledgements   133

      Index   134

FOREWORD

There are many books about buildings, but few about builders. In fact Hermione Hobhouse's classic study of the London builder Thomas Cubitt is the only one that comes readily to mind. The publication of this history of a well-known Oxford firm of builders is therefore very much to be welcomed.

Unlike Cubitt, Daniel Evans and his successors rarely engaged in speculative building, and then only on the smallest scale. Throughout its history, the profits of the firm that he founded early in the nineteenth century have been derived chiefly from the regular employment afforded by the collegiate university of Oxford. Whereas Cubitt built chiefly in London stock brick, Symm, like their rivals Knowles, built chiefly in stone, at first from local quarries and Bath, then from Clipsham, and in recent years from as far afield as France. It is due to the skill of their masons that many of the most admired buildings of Oxford are still standing today, and this carefully compiled record of the firm and its work is a valuable contribution to the history both of the city and of the building industry.

Howard Colvin St. John's College
Oxford

The President & Gentlemen of Magdalen
     College — — — — — — — — — — — — Dᴿ £ .. s .. d

Contract for new Magdalen Hall — — — — — 7929 . 0 . 0
Repairs of the Old Buildings of Hertford College
     to Xmas 1821 — — — — — — — — — 1204 .. 16 . 8
Cementing the Outside of the Chapel — — — — 139 . 6 . 0
Extra Foundation to the Kitchen & Boundry Wall
     in College Lane — — — — — — — — 95 . 10 . 0
Bill of Extra's — — — — — — — — — — 529 . 17 . 9½
Sinking & Steining the Well — — — — — — 30 . 5 . 0
Extra Foundation as Measur'd by Mr Garbot — 476 .. 1 .. 6
Bell hanging in the Principals House — — — 28 . 0 . 0
Bright Stove to the Dining Hall — — — — — 10 . 0 . 0
Preparing Ground & Seeds for Grass — — — — 2 . 10 . 0
Mens Dinner at the Raising — — — — — — 5 . 0 . 0

                            £ 10450 .. 6 .. 11½

Work done at the Old Magdalen Hall
     as p Bill deliver'd — — — — — — 123 . 12 . 5
Ditto — Magdalen College — — — — 469 . 10 . 6½
Bill of Painting & Admitted by
     Mr Parkinson — — — — — — 104 . 13 . 0
Magdalen College Bill to the
     13ᵗʰ of Janʸ 1823 — — — } 18 . 4 . 10

                            716 . 0 . 9½

                          £ 11166 .. 7 .. 9

INTRODUCTION

David Sturdy

Builders, Architects and Clients

Daniel Evans

In 1820 Daniel Evans began his first college contract, the twin west blocks of Magdalen Hall (now Hertford College) in Catte Street, the first major new college building in Oxford for thirty years. He had a particularly complex task, to satisfy the architect and three different customers, one of them his immediate client, the second, the source of funds and the third, the central University authorities. He was most successful in all these respects; he built up useful long term links with all three customers and also established himself as the city's first general contractor, employing his own teams of workmen in the different branches of the trade.

The architect on the job, William Garbett, failed to make any such fruitful impression and, like many other architects summoned to Oxford for a specific task, left no other significant mark on the place. He was Surveyor to Winchester Cathedral without a base or any experience of working in Oxford; that Cathedral has three spectacular memorial chapels to Oxford college founders and he may have won the commission by repairing one.

The immediate client was Dr. J.D. Macbride, appointed in 1813 to preside over Magdalen Hall's transference from a congested location close beside the gate of Magdalen College to the new site. Macbride, who had been an undergraduate and fellow of Exeter, was also professor of Arabic; unusually for an Oxford college head at that time, he was not a clergyman. As Principal of a Hall, he had absolute authority over his tutors and did not have to take account of a governing body of fellows. In his time student numbers rose to over two hundred, four times as many as at Magdalen College. A vigorous evangelical he had a good deal of sympathy with Methodists like his builder and had helped reduce the considerable debt left after Evans built the second Methodist chapel in New Inn Hall Street by purchasing its predecessor.

The funds to build in Catte Street came, not from any fund-raising effort by Macbride on the Hall's behalf, but from its former neighbour, Magdalen College, anxious to enlarge its already vast site. Unlike the Hall which had a few endowed scholarships but no general endowment, the College had a large endowed income from its ancient estates across the south of England, including many houses in the city centre. This was not efficiently managed and the College accounts, rigidly audited in obedience to the Founder's statutes, had to conform to a medieval format under twenty-four largely

opposite page:
Magdalen College account book, detailing work carried out by Daniel Evans, 1821

9

Magdalen Hall, 1822

irrelevant headings. Dr. M.J. Routh, the scholarly President of Magdalen, has been castigated for being 'painfully timid' in architectural debate and unable to secure agreement over the College's own building projects. He made no attempt to dominate his restless and pushy Fellows; but he did control a New Building fund, set up a hundred years earlier to circumvent the archaic accounting system. The College was pleased enough with the new Magdalen Hall to have kept Garbett's plans with its own large collection of abortive designs. Evans impressed them too. He was called in to work there as soon as the College had half made up its mind.

The University itself had allowed the old Hertford College to die out so that Magdalen Hall could take over the site and had bought and emptied the houses on the street front. This process dragged on from 1813 to 1820 while four Vice-Chancellors held sway. They were then college heads who took the office in turn: Dr. Cole of Exeter College, Dr. Lee of Trinity, Dr. Hodson of Brasenose and Dr. Hall of Pembroke. Daniel Evans made useful contacts which led to work at Pembroke and Exeter.

While he was completing the Magdalen Hall blocks, Evans was involved in a curious piratical exploit with his second client, Magdalen College. In August 1822 he led a pre-dawn demolition squad of a hundred men there on the orders of a faction or group of Fellows intent on direct action in the depths of the Long Vacation, while everyone was away. In one morning they tore down most of the north range of the medieval cloisters, only to be told forcibly that they were acting without proper authority. Edward Ellerton, a stalwart low-churchman and Senior Fellow, arrived unexpectedly and halted the workmen before they were able to wreck the east range too.

The full story of this fantastic escapade has never been told. Magdalen had for decades dreamed of ambitious building projects, but had never been able to decide on any one of several dozen designs commissioned from leading architects or submitted by hopefuls. It is unclear which of several architects was most involved; even President Routh's role is obscure and was perhaps ambivalent. In July 1822 the college had voted to accept a scheme by the artist and antiquary John Buckler, but the London architect, Joseph Parkinson, was also called in to declare the structure dangerous and it was his coarse and repetitive late-gothic design that was used for the north and east sides of the cloisters. Through this remarkable series of squabbles, intrigues and changes of plan, Evans remained in favour at Magdalen College, though he was not one of the regular maintenance builders called in every year. As related in this history he carried out over £10,000 worth of rebuilding there in 1824-26. But Parkinson was never employed in Oxford again and his contribution to the Oxford scene can be seen as an example of 'too many cooks...'.

In 1829 Dr. Hall, a 'little mild man' who was vice-chancellor when Evans was building the twin Magdalen Hall blocks, called on him to redesign Pembroke, which had no spare income to hurl into lavish rebuilding on the scale of Magdalen. Evans refaced and raised the street-front in a startling late-gothic style and refaced the quad with simple and economical mock-Tudor details. Dr. Hall presided over the change; Evans made his own designs directly expressing Hall's character in the quad, but the street-front may owe more to his autocratic deputy Charles Wightwick, Vice-Gerent of the college.

Every building carries a message, some very complex. It is always challenging and fascinating to work out how far a great work of architecture expresses the character of its creator. In almost every case, as we have seen, it needs careful enquiry to find whose personality, the builder, his client or the designer, whether architect or draughtsman, had most influence. Sometimes the main influence was the fashion of the age.

In 1828-29, just before he turned to Pembroke, Daniel Evans was able to please himself when he designed and built a group of three houses in St. Giles', No. 34 to live in himself and Nos. 35 and 36 to let. He could walk down his back garden, open the gate at the end, and step straight into his yard; very much a new kind of businessman, he was not a pioneer commuter. The whole group, set back from the pavement to allow room for an area, is nine bays long and three storeys high with attics and basements. The three houses stand in a wide part of the street, where the Woodstock and Banbury Roads diverge and are designed to catch the eye from eighty yards away. They formed a terrace of the kind that had been built in many parts of London in compliance with the Building Act of 1774, but faced with Bath stone instead

*Pembroke College
(Oxford Almanack 1838)*

of brick or stucco. The attic windows have round tops rising behind a pierced parapet; the second floor windows are plain without moulded surrounds; the first floor has surrounds and a balcony with delicately detailed balustrading and lions' heads; the ground floor is rusticated and the three front doorways, double-stepped in section, have semicircular fanlights with central circles and rounded comet-shaped divisions with pointed tails or 'mouchettes' while fleur-de-lys top the cast iron fence. Evans designed these houses with rich, if rather conventional, decoration to attract tenants and as an advertisement to show what he could do.

A few years later, in 1831-32, and two hundred and fifty yards away he built another group of three houses, Nos. 20-22 St. John Street. They are the same size as the St. Giles' houses, but much plainer, meant to be seen across a fairly narrow street from no more than forty feet away. They rise from the pavement without an area and are three storeys high with attics and basements. They have no front fence and no rustication, no window-surrounds and no balcony, no pierced parapet and flat-topped attic windows. There are distinctive characteristics in the three doorways with the same double-stepped section and similar fanlights with central circles and comet-shaped divisions as in St. Giles'. Daniel Evans built these houses with very different aims and under constraints. They had to follow the general design which St. John's College, the ground landlord, had imposed; and Evans never planned to live there. As soon as he had completed them, he advertised them for sale in the local paper.

Another of Evans' contracts carries yet another kind of message. Francis

Jeune, a leading Evangelical from the Channel Islands, succeeded Dr. Hall as Master of Pembroke in April 1844. In the 1830s, as headmaster of King Edward's, Birmingham, he had revived, reformed, and rebuilt the school to the designs of Charles Barry, a promising and well-travelled London architect. Within a year of his arrival, Pembroke had the sixth largest intake of students at Oxford, rising to the fourth largest within five years. By November 1844 the college, one of the poorest, had approved plans and managed to raise loans and donations for extensive new buildings to house the increased student intake. Barry was now famous, having won the competition for the Houses of Parliament in 1836.

Badly overworked, he passed Jeune to his nephew, Charles Hayward of Exeter, whose simple gothic design for Pembroke, partly carried out by Daniel Evans, is a symbol of Jeune's contacts with government circles in London. The large scale of the new buildings represents Jeune's personal determination and ambition for his college, for change and for reform. In 1850 he was the only college head to serve on the Royal Commission on Oxford University, whose other members and supporters had a crucial impact on the appearance of Oxford and the fortunes of Symm and Co. But like Garbett and Parkinson, Hayward secured no other commissions at Oxford.

Joshua R. Symm

When Joshua Symm took over the business in 1846 he was able to continue what had become the firm's main work, constructing a good proportion of all large new college buildings. He was involved in new extensions, drastic rebuilding and regular maintenance and repair, particularly at Exeter College in 1854 and from 1863 to 1881 at Christ Church. Here he met the firm's greatest patron, Henry Liddell, the outstanding college head of the 19th century, when he won the contact to build Meadow Buildings. Dean Liddell left much for us to remember him by, from the City's main sewers to the New Cut (the present mouth of the Cherwell); from *Liddell and Scott* his Greek/English lexicon which has been in print through countless revisions and editions since 1843; to *Alice in Wonderland*, first told to entertain daughters by one of his College tutors on a river-picnic in 1863. He was the 'true founder and friend' of the Society of Unattached Students, which has become St. Catherine's College; he also supported the School of Art which was to form one of the founding elements of the Oxford Brookes University. He played a leading part in the University reforms of the 1850s and created the Governing Body of his own college in the 1860s. With Symm as his builder and designs from three successive architects he extended, rebuilt and restored the college into very much the form we still see today over a century later. Liddell's impact on Christ Church was immense.

As a minor boom in college-building in the 1850s rose to a high peak in the 1880s, two major architectural firms outside Oxford competed for the most prestigious commissions, often winning them from local men. Symm worked successfully with both firms and their clients, and was always able to survive a change of architect.

George Gilbert Scott (1811-1878) had made his name as a gothic designer in Oxford in 1840 when he won the competition for the Martyrs Memorial. Turning from workhouses, his previous speciality, to cathedral restoration and church-building generally he built up a huge practice with many assistants and pupils. Based in central London, he was the most successful and prolific architect in the country, building new churches by the dozen while also moving on to great public buildings and grand London railway stations.

Scott's twenty Oxford commissions, bold and coarsely detailed, stand out pugnaciously, differing from their neighbours in scale and visual rhythm. They were commissioned by reforming college heads and fellows, linked by an intriguing network of school and college connections, as powerful symbols of the changes which they had imposed and intended to impose on the easy-going, complacent old university. In 1854 Exeter College commissioned him to complete its Broad Street front, half-built by Evans in the 1830s to designs by Underwood. This led onto the rebuilding of much of the college, including the spectacular chapel, all designed by Scott and built by Symm. For the next twenty-five years, Scott was constantly busy in Oxford, often visiting the place himself. For much of this time, twenty-two years, Symm was his regular contractor. As well as Exeter, Symm built the Library and Buttery and

Exeter College: Broad Street front

restored the Chapel at University College, all to Scott's designs, for a reforming Master, F.C. Plumptre, in 1859-63.

Scott's main rival was the Dublin firm of Deane and Woodward, later Sir Thomas Deane and Son, whose Oxford début came through a protracted competition for the University Museum (of Natural History) that lasted for much of 1854, the year of Scott's Exeter commission. From 1855 to 1886, with a short break in 1861-62 and a much longer one in 1872-83, Deane and Woodward were busy in Oxford. They carried out nine commissions for the University itself, for the Union Debating Society and for Christ Church, the largest and wealthiest college, where in due course they were supplanted by Scott. J.R. Symm and his successor company, Symm and Co., won the contracts for most of these prestigious buildings.

At Christ Church H.G. Liddell, Dean of Christ Church from 1855, had served with Jeune of Pembroke on the Commission to reform the university while he was Headmaster of Westminster. A London contractor, Baker's of Lambeth was his first choice for renovating his official residence, the Deanery in Tom Quad in 1855-56. The college had been accumulating a building-fund for

Bird's eye view of Exeter College, 1859

decades; Liddell soon spent it and much more besides on a grandiose rebuilding of an old and humble part of the college, the Chaplains' Quadrangle and the adjoining Fell's Building as Meadow Buildings, built by Symm in 1863-66 to Deane and Woodward's design.

Over the next fifteen years Symm's men were never absent from Christ Church as they overhauled almost every aspect of the fabric, under the guidance of Liddell and generally to the plans of Scott, who replaced Deane in circumstances which have not yet been fully revealed. Together they replaced the balustrade originally placed round Tom Quad in the 1660s with the present battlements and pinnacles and undertook the great restoration of the Cathedral in 1870-76.

1874: Symm and Co.

Soon after 1874, when he went into partnership with his clerk Howard, foreman mason Axtell and foreman joiner Hart, J.R. Symm (who died in 1887) and his Partners began the firm's long association with the Bodleian Library, while they continued with the great works at Christ Church and lesser projects throughout Oxford. In 1876 they embarked on what was to prove a nine-year programme of stone repairs at the Bodleian, the University's central library, whose buildings were part-medieval and part-Jacobean. Most builders have probably, and quite naturally, tended to shift from construction to repair and maintenance, often called back by satisfied clients. At this time Symm and Co. achieved this same transition, establishing a pattern which has continued for well over a century until today.

Throughout this period they have very successfully kept a balance between

The Cathedral, Christ Church: restoration of tower and spire

The Hall and Wolsey Tower, Christ Church, with building work in foreground (Oxford Almanack 1881)

new construction and maintenance, often of college and university buildings they had originally built. That balance has been a matter of business judgement. The firm's longevity, however, has depended as much on its leadership and management, from one generation to the next, its continued commitment to the highest standards of workmanship and its absolute concern for its reputation. All this is recorded in the historical account which follows.

Oxford, 1817

CHAPTER

THE OXFORD BUILDING TRADE

Oxford, special and indeed unique as it was, grew substantially but did not share in the explosive growth exhibited by many British towns in the nineteenth century. It was not an Oldham or a Wolverhampton, nor indeed a Northampton or a Reading. Its population grew from 11,921 in 1801 to 27,843 in 1851 and say 53,000 by 1911; in the same period Oldham, for instance, grew from 12,000 to 147,000.

The size of the building trade - measured by those employed as masons, bricklayers, carpenters, plasterers, painters, plumbers, glaziers and other craftsmen, and the more amorphous group of associated labourers - would be related to population size. It was the size and growth of a town that would mainly govern its demand for houses, and public buildings such as churches, town halls, public offices, market halls, schools or hospitals. And yet Oxford had a far larger building trade than at any time its population size and growth would indicate.

The point can be illustrated from the Census returns for 1851. Excluding labourers, Oxford had 861 men engaged in the building trades of whom 281 were carpenters and 242 masons; Northampton, a town of similar size, had only 594, including 202 carpenters and 121 masons. This disparity was maintained at subsequent Censuses; Oxford continued to employ far more carpenters, masons, plasterers and glaziers, but not bricklayers. The explanation for the contrast lay in Oxford's obvious characteristic: the presence of the University and its colleges with their unique heritage of historic buildings in stone, revered and precious, often the work of the most distinguished architects and builders of the time. The care of these buildings and the need to modify them, and to add to them as the University grew in size and extended its activities, created a separate building market in Oxford which had its own special features. Oxford, in other words, had two building markets, that of the town and that of the University. To some extent those markets merged, to some extent they were distinct. The enterprises and work force which made up the building trades would service both markets but in most cases would specialise in one rather than the other.

The buildings of the University and its colleges dated from the Mediaeval and Tudor to the Restoration and Georgian periods. Their age alone created

opposite page:
The Hall, Christ Church: stonework in progress, 1900s
(Oxford Almanack, 1918)

an ongoing demand for maintenance and repair. To that the nineteenth century brought the need for enlargement, modernisation and replacement. As undergraduate populations grew, if only modestly, additional accommodation was needed; more importantly a higher standard of accommodation with less sharing of rooms gave another imperative to enlargement. Similarly the accommodation of fellows was upgraded. All this meant new buildings and new quadrangles; lecture rooms, libraries, common rooms all had to be enlarged, replaced or brought to a better standard. Chapels and halls, in many cases, were refurbished or replaced with more modern buildings. The house of the college head, the master's lodgings as it might be termed, important in the place of things, accommodating a large household of family, relatives, guests and servants, was a frequent subject of new college building. In all cases there was an ongoing need for modernisation, mundane requirements such as drains and flush lavatories, baths, hot water heating, electric light, better kitchens and the like. The expansion of the University had other consequences. Some new colleges were built the most notable example being Keble, and later the first women's colleges, but large new University buildings were an important need especially the Examination Schools, an enlarged Bodleian Library and the whole complex of the Science Area with its Museum and specialised buildings and laboratories.

Finally the decay of the stone fabric of the historic buildings, a function of the characteristics of the local limestone originally employed, age and eventually pollution, dictated the need for restoration and replacement. This huge and delicate task particularly applied to some of the precious central buildings such as the Clarendon Building, the Ashmolean and above all the Bodleian Library as well as to many of the older college buildings. Important as this work was in the later nineteenth century, it became an even larger challenge across the University after the Second World War.

This then was the University market, completely unlike the market say for working class or suburban housing, offices or shops. The clientele, the University and college authorities, dons and their advisers could be difficult and demanding. Given their obsessive concern, pleasing them and the college *alumni*, frequently men of great distinction, was an exacting requirement. They were not always well endowed with funds for building, relying heavily on benefactions, and at times they were slow payers, however reliable in the end. But rightly their standards were high; the buildings that were being modified, replaced or extended were a unique heritage; compatible harmonious style was essential and controversial. Above all sensitive workmanship of the highest standard, executed unobtrusively, reliably, and efficiently, was the prime requirement for a college builder. When it came to

Quarry men excavating the raw material that has shaped Oxford's unique characteristic over the centuries

new buildings, extensions or major restoration the colleges searched for distinction and accordingly the foremost architects of the day were engaged; men such as Gilbert Scott, Jackson, Waterhouse and Butterfield. They would have their own strong views about building and builders and to succeed a local builder would need to develop a confident relationship with them. All these architects preferred to work with building firms they knew whenever they could, firms that could be expected to finish on time and were financially sound. They were demanding to work for with a sharp eye for quality, but if they liked a builder they were loyal to him.

What of the Oxford building trades which supplied this University, and the general town building demand? The early nineteenth century directories identify a number of specialist craft businesses, bricklayers, masons, carpenters, plasterers and so on. This reflected practice up to this time: a building project would be put out to a lead master craftsman, most typically a bricklayer, mason or a carpenter; he would use his own workforce to carry out his speciality but sub-contract the remainder of the work to other specialist enterprises, slaters, plasterers, plumbers and so forth, co-ordinating, supervising and assuming responsibility for the whole, and charging a fee or taking a profit on the value of the sub-contracted work. Such a system implied close collaboration between the specialist firms, each of them small jobbing employers. As the century progressed, this system evolved into that of the building contractor, specialising or not as the case might be on particular types of work. A building contractor, or a builder as he would be called, would employ a range of wage-earning craftsmen providing the range of skills needed to carry out a complete project; sometimes he might continue to sub-contract some specialist work, the plumbing and the glazing perhaps, usually to close and trusted associates. The head of a successful building firm would have expert knowledge of particular trades, in Oxford usually stonemasonry and stonework, the ability to manage a workforce, and commercial skills involved in negotiating contracts and maintaining good relations with demanding clients in a competitive business situation. Such a firm was competent to do everything necessary in a project from beginning to end. The builder would usually work for a firm price and on a large project, carried out to an architect's designs and specifications, the building works would be supervised by a clerk of works who would monitor quality. The architect would approve stage payments as the work progressed, authorise extras and variations. The builder might be required to provide a bond or surety to protect his client.

Of the Oxford college builders in the mid-nineteenth century a number of firms were prominent. Evans and Symm, of course, but also the long established Thomas Knowles of Holywell and Margaret Wyatt of St. Giles' competed with each other but also had their individual steady college clientele; Robert Castle and John Plowman were others. These firms, provided they maintained their reputation, had a more secure market than building firms generally. Reputation for skilled craftsmanship and reliable service was crucial. In the general building market competition was intense, partly because the barriers to entry were low. A time-served skilled man could readily find the wherewithal to start on his own; capital requirements were small, credit on materials would be available and to some extent working capital, needed principally to finance land purchases and pay labour, could be borrowed from banks and other sources of finance such as building societies. But this was a precarious vitality and the mortality of firms was high, primarily because the market was unstable, margins low and default or inability to sell houses built speculatively not uncommon. Many small firms lacked the experience or standing to order timber, stone, glass, slates and bricks and the like advantageously. These hazards were less severe for the college builders. Apart from maintenance of their capital, the main factor in their longevity would be the ability to manage the succession from one generation to the next. Finding family or associates with the commitment and skill to understand and manage the business was not always assured. Management and commercial ability was not enough; the principals had to have the expertise in their trade and in stone and stonework in particular; they had to be able to hold together a team of skilled craftsmen not merely by providing steady work at acceptable wages but by example and leadership. Among the Oxford builders Symm and Knowles have both been exceptional in their longevity, the former through six generations of principals.

Much of the everyday work done for colleges was so-called daywork where time and materials, precisely calculated, were charged. On restoration projects measured work was the rule, with agreed charges per cubic foot of stonework depending on its complexity, pinnacles for instance considerably more than ashlar. On large building works tenders were invited and building firms would prepare detailed estimates, an important task for the principals and a necessary part of their overheads; here they were committed to do the whole work for a firm price.

Of all the great industries in the nineteenth century, building was the least affected by machinery and technical advance. The craft skills, methods and tools of stone working or carpentry remained as they had been for centuries. Craftsmen found their own tools, often costing £5 to £10 a set. Blocks of stone were sawn by huge hand saws and stone was then further cut, dressed and worked, all entirely by hand. Banker masons

Sawn blocks of stone outside Banker Masons' shop

and fixer masons had their respective traditional roles. Time honoured seven year apprenticeships governed entry to the ranks of skilled men. Eventually steam winches might drive hoists, or power driven stone and timber saws be introduced; steel tube might replace pole scaffolding; motor driven trucks take the place of horse and cart. But change was slow, tradition, custom and practice had a firm hold.

At mid-century most of the building firms in Oxford were very small. The 1851 Census suggests that Knowles, for instance, employed six men; Matthew, also in Holywell, fifteen and Hope nine men and a live-in apprentice. Many identified as builders or specialist tradesmen were no more than father and son or sons with perhaps one or two men, time-served journeymen and perhaps an apprentice. The largest firms at the time were Henry Cowley, Clarendon Buildings, with eighteen men, as well as four sons, all carpenters; James Gardner in George Street with twenty-two men; Wyatt in Magdalen Street with twenty men. Symm did not record his workforce at the time, although both in 1851 and 1861 there were a cluster of masons, carpenters and the like living near to his yard in Little Clarendon Street and the streets close by.

As the century grew older, the successful firms became larger, even substantial employers, with up to 150 or 200 employees at seasonal/activity peaks. All these enterprises had their premises or yards close to the city centre and the University buildings and colleges where their work took place. On larger projects, towards the end of the century, where competitions were held and tenders invited, outside building firms found a foothold in the Oxford market, and some, such as Parnell of Rugby or Estcourt of Gloucester, for instance, did a great deal of work over the years. Artistic work, sculpture, finely carved stone or woodwork, stained glass, tiled mosaic, would typically be carried out by specialist London firms rather than the Oxford trade

Within the college sector, the demand for building work was not uniform. So far as the University and the colleges were concerned there

The traditional horse and cart

Hunt's Oxford Directory of 1846

DIRECTORY.]	OXFORD.	57

(Glovers only)
Richings Ann, 17, St. Clement st.
Ridley Christopher. 12, Holywell street

Brewers.
Marked thus * are Retail Brewers.
Archer John, St. Aldate street
*Blencowe John, Red Lion sq.
*Evans Joel, Cowley road
*Farbrother Edwd. 2, Walton pl.
Hall Henry, & Tawney Charles & Co. Saint Thomas's
*Hall Elizabeth, Observatory st.
*Miller Wm. Church street
Morrell James, Senr. St. Thomas's
*Painton Wm. Friars Entry
Parker John, St. Clement's

Builders.
Barrett John, Lit. Clarendon st.
Barrett Thomas, Observatory st.
Bartlett Wm. 9, New road
Carter John, 4, New College lane
Castle Robert & John, Cowley rd.
Chaundy John. Littlegate
Evans Dan. & Symm J. Robinson Little Clarendon street
Fisher Wm. St. Ebbe street
Gardiner James, 8, George street
Hope Joseph, 35, Holywell street
Hudson John, & Matthew John, Long Wall street
Johnson James, Walton place
Jones Thomas, 63, George street
King Alf. Cherwell st St. Clemt's
Knight Wm. 21, Queen street
Liddell Robert, 22. St. Clement st
Ludlow Stephen, St. Aldate st.
Noon Thomas, Jericho
Plowman John, & Luck Isaac, 12. Merton street
Quarterman Henry, St. Aldate st.
Redhead Richard, 33, Broad st.
Tomkins Thos. 16, Magdalene st,
Walter James, 4, Lit Clarendon st
Winterborne Thomas, Blenheim pl
Wyatt Margaret. St. Giles' street

Butchers.
Alden John, 13, Walton place
Alden Thomas, Abingdon road
Andrews Andrew, Observatory st.
Andrews Wm. Hen. Blackfriars rd
Baker Joseph, Speedwell street
Bolton Fred. Wm. St. Clement st.
Brain Wm. St. Thomas's
Bryan John, Jericho
Claridge James, Jericho
Collins Edward, 27, St Aldate st.
Eaton Charles, 62, George street
Faulkner John, 35, St. Aldate st.
Harper James, Jericho
Jessop John, Paradise street
Lewin Wm. 25, St. Aldate street
Loder Mary, Cowley road
Mansfield Thomas, Church street
Marsh Thomas. 42, George street
Mobley Geo. 29, Observatory st.
Mobley Wm Friar street
Price John, 8, St. Ebbe street
Price, Wm. St. Giles
Solloway Daniel, Church street
Solloway Thomas, Jericho
Stevens Jno. & Geo. 19, Holywell street
Tustin Sam. Calcutt, 8, St.Giles st.
Walklett Thomas, Jericho
Wiblin Chas. St. Clement street
Wiblin John, St. Clement street
Wilkins Chas. St. Clement street
Woodford Chas. Church street
Woodford Geo. 16, Bull street
Wyatt Robert, St. Clement's

Butchers, (Pork) and Bacon Curers.
Adams John A. Commercial road
Birt John, 7, Park end street
Birt Thomas, Jericho
Bowell Thomas, 33, George street
Cooper Richard, St. Clement st.
Cowley James, St. Thomas street
Faulkner Charles, Jericho
Hughes Saml. 20, St. Clement st.
Loder Wm. St. Clement street
Mobley John, Walton terrace
Moss Sarah, St. Thomas street

were strong phases of expansion and restoration, and quieter phases. The business cycle would apply; in extended periods of bad trade and economic depression college funds would be strained as rental income or endowments fell, although the general building market would be more directly affected. College work was especially carried out in the Long Vacation, curtailed in term time. Outdoor work was seasonal, depending on temperature, rain, frost and snow, as well as the hours of daylight; winters were invariably slack, although plumbers were in demand in the periods of hard frost. In the busy periods in the summer long spells of overtime were common, eagerly accepted by the men for their extra earnings.

Not surprisingly although activity and income in the building trades were unstable, the workforce took much of this instability. If hours of work were reduced, earnings fell. If there was little work then numbers employed fell. Men, skilled men as well as labourers, were laid off. They might remain unemployed until other work often with a different employer came up, living off savings, borrowings, what could be picked up from casual jobs, or outdoor poor relief *in extremis*. They might drift into other occupations or, commonly enough, move to other districts where work was available or migrate to lands overseas where opportunity beckoned. A surplus pool of labour, skilled and unskilled, was the normal situation. Only the best workmen had any degree of security. This was the nineteenth century labour market with the hazards of sickness, unemployment or old age, protected inadequately by friendly societies or in the last resort the Guardians and the workhouse.

In Oxford itself there were many tradesmen supplying the colleges and their don and undergraduate populations with food and drink, clothing and footwear, books, printed matter, furnishings and so on. And there were college servants, predominantly male, not well paid and certainly in the early nineteenth century often not paid at all in the vacations, but following an occupation which had status and dignity and security. Work in the colleges was sought after; sons followed their fathers and dynasties of college servants were not unknown. But tradesmen and college servants apart, work in nineteenth century Oxford was not plentiful and there was 'a background of low wages to the labour of the place'. Wages were not high in the building trade, not as high as in London or the manufacturing towns. This was true even for the skilled men, masons and carpenters and painters, who having served their time, might be earning 25 shillings or 30 shillings in the mid century; 30 shillings to 35 shillings by the 1880s or 7½ pence an hour. Apprenticeship, bound by firm rules, remained essential in these trades. Labourers were poorly paid, perhaps 3 shillings a day or 4 pence for the hour; boys and lads got 5 shillings a week. In periods of bad trade wages would be cut.

Hours of work were long, at least when daylight permitted. They would be set by custom but unregulated so far as overtime was concerned. From 70 hours weekly in the early nineteenth century, they had settled to 58 to 60 hours by the late 1850s and there they remained until the late century, 10 hours or so a day during the week and a Saturday that finished early, that is at 4 o'clock. By the 1880s when Saturday work finished at mid-day, hours were then 54 in summer, 50 in winter. Throughout the century work started at 6 o'clock in the morning, daylight permitting. Men had to walk to their work wherever it might be at the time. This was a rough trade: discipline was fairly harsh; foremen were typically 'drivers' and poor workers were readily sacked. In Oxford trade unions were not active and a man like Joshua Symm would have a strict but personal and direct relationship with each of his regular men. Being a builder could be a dangerous occupation and accidents were not infrequent. There was one compensation - the feasts provided for workmen by patrons on the occasion of 'topping out', that is completing the highest point, as well as finishing the entire project. Ample fare, roast beef, plum pudding, with plenty of strong ale and tobacco, speeches and songs provided memorable occasions, a perk of the job.

Poor wages and insecurity seemed to have encouraged both working wives and large families. Children from early in their lives were a source of family income. Wives also found ways of earning. One of Symm's foremen ran a shop as a second occupation; taking in washing, child-minding, dress-making were other sources of income. As the century grew older, living standards improved not so much because of higher wages as because the cost of living fell, and a wider range of foods and comforts became available. Beer was always cheap and remained a mainstay for the building trades worker. Craftsmen and certainly labourers, lived for the most part close to the City centre, the markets and their places of employment, in the working class districts of St. Ebbe's and Jericho and in the parish of Holy Trinity near the gas works and the river

Such was the Oxford building trade in which Daniel Evans and his successors Joshua Symm and the Axtell dynasty developed and maintained a successful business over two centuries.

THE FOUNDATIONS: 1815-1846
DANIEL EVANS, FOUNDER

Daniel Evans was born about 1769, probably in Fairford, Gloucestershire. He was apparently apprenticed for seven years to James Adams, upholsterer of 20, High Street, Oxford. Where he acquired his building skills and worked as a young man is obscure. Certainly he moved about the country since his only daughter was born in Bolton, Lancashire in 1804. Subsequently he was living at 37, Eagle Street, Holborn, in central London where he was one of several active builders established in that neighbourhood, among them the young Thomas Cubitt (1788-1855).

Evans became a Methodist and this led to his involvement with the Revd. William Jenkins (1763-1844), a Methodist minister who in 1810 had set up as an architect and lived nearby in Red Lion Square, Holborn. Jenkins designed several Methodist chapels at this period, in London and elsewhere.

The Wesleyan Chapel in Leicester, built by Daniel Evans in 1815

Thus to Jenkins' plans, in 1815 Daniel Evans built the Wesleyan Chapel in Bishop Street, Leicester, a large building with galleries, seating more than a thousand, and costing about £4,900. This was followed in the same year by the Gold Street Chapel in Northampton, opened in January 1816. Evans would be accustomed to carry out such projects outside London, lodging near the site of the building with his key craftsman, engaging local labour but contracting out other work to specialist tradesmen, perhaps the carpentry,

Evans' Leicester Chapel today, 1998

the roofing, the plastering and painting. Evans' own trade had become that of a bricklayer and his closest associates were probably stonemasons.

The Methodists in Oxford asked William Jenkins to design a chapel on a site they had acquired along New Inn Hall Street in the centre of the City. This building, commenced in 1816 and completed the following year, was Daniel Evans' first Oxford venture. The new chapel, costing £2,965 to build, would attract attention and certainly create awareness of the name and competence of the builder. It may have led to Evans' next commission.

The first Oxford venture: the Wesleyan Chapel in New Inn Hall Street, completed in 1817

Dr. John Macbride, appointed Principal of Magdalen Hall within the University in 1813, although an evangelical Anglican, had some sympathy and connection with the Methodist congregation and bought their previous chapel, which was probably in debt, in 1818. Perhaps it was because of the Methodist connection he met Evans who was engaged for what became the new buildings of Magdalen Hall, some of their previous buildings having been destroyed by a fire in January 1820. Magdalen College jumped at the chance to move its humbler offshoot, Magdalen Hall, which had developed out of the College's grammar school, to the site left vacant by the collapse of the first Hertford College. To get rid of the Hall, Magdalen College cheerfully paid for its new buildings on the Hertford site in Catte Street.

William Garbett of Winchester was architect for the new buildings; Evans had to give some form of security for fulfilling his contract as builder, perhaps not unusual at the time. Following a procession of Magdalen College Fellows and the Principal and others of Magdalen Hall, in which the builder, Mr. Evans, 'bore the level', the foundation stone was ceremonially laid by the Vice-President of Magdalen on 3 May 1820. The new buildings were completed in 1822 and a print survives showing the Catte Street Front as it then appeared; the front did not escape criticism and an Oxford man in 1847 described it as 'a barbarous modern building.' The two classically formal square blocks - the northern one being undergraduate rooms and the other, the Principal's Lodgings - were joined by a stone screen in the middle of which was an archway. The building of a new Dining-Hall in 1887, for what had by then adopted the name of Hertford College, changed the archway but the blocks remain, simple and severe, faced as the specification stated with 'known

Preparing the site for Magdalen Hall about 1819. In the background across Catte Street is the Radcliffe Camera and the Bodleian (Oxford Almanack 1825)

stone of the neighbourhood.' This was a substantial contract for as much as £7,929 to which extras including repairs to the old buildings of Hertford College were added, bringing the total to £10,450. The College paid £5 for men's dinners at the raising which would suggest as many as 50 men were employed. At least in part Evans was paid by Bills of Exchange which would suggest that the Hall lacked cash, as would not be unusual. He credited the Hall with the value of the old stone which he took to use elsewhere.

Evans' work at Magdalen Hall was succeeded by a large programme of building and restoration at Magdalen College itself, in part under the London architect, Joseph Parkinson. Over a period of five years 1822-27, Evans was responsible for additions to the much admired Georgian New Buildings of

The Catte Street front of Magdalen Hall, completed by Evans in 1822. Twenty five years later it was described as 'a barbarous modern building'

The New Building, MAGDALEN COLLEGE from the Grove.

The New Building at Magdalen College: in the 1820s wings were added, which are shown in this engraving.

1733, and repairs to the fifteenth century Chapel, Cloister Quadrangle, Dining Hall and Library where the roof was raised and interior refurbished. This extensive work at Magdalen, highly sensitive as it would be, was the subject of dispute and controversy between the College authorities, the builder and the various architects. The College History may be quoted on what took place:

'the roof, and indeed the whole fabric, of the north and east fronts of the Cloister Quadrangle were in a dangerous condition.... The whole of the north front was actually pulled down in 1822. The work...hastily pushed on by a builder employed by the College, without full authority, was stopped before...rebuilding...had proceeded very far, and for some time the College was the battleground of contending architects who poured forth more or less impossible designs for rebuilding, altering, or completing this and other portions of the buildings. It was at last decided that the north front should be rebuilt on the old lines. This work was carried out in 1824 and was followed in 1825 and 1826 by the rebuilding of the rooms on the east side of the Quadrangle and in 1827 by the rebuilding of the south cloister.'

North Front of the College facing the New Building.

The north side of Cloister Quadrangle at Magdalen College before and after rebuilding in the 1820s

A Design for improving the present North Front by the addition of Gables at the extremities and the removal of the unsightly garret windows.
The Bow Window would be an elegant and ornamental appendage to the Library, and the restoration of the other Windows will render this Design very handsome.

33

Engraving of the completed Radcliffe Asylum c1833, now the Warneford Hospital

THE RADCLIFFE ASYLUM, ON HEADINGTON HILL.

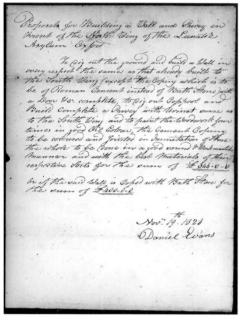

Evans' estimate for a wall and privy at the Asylum

Evans would have been at the centre of this controversy. Still living in London at the outset of the work, he appears to have rented a small dwelling in Oxford. While he did not escape criticism, he was retained to complete the whole programme for which he was paid £20,484. His reputation seems to have taken no harm.

Before the work at Magdalen had begun, Evans had already won the contract for a major civic project, namely the Radcliffe Asylum (now the Warneford Hospital), financed by a number of benefactors. A site was found in Headington parish, designs prepared by Richard Ingleman of Southwell, Nottinghamshire, who had previous experience in designing asylums, and the tender advertised in May 1821. Evans' successful application undertook to build the centre block and south wing for £7,250 with an agreement to

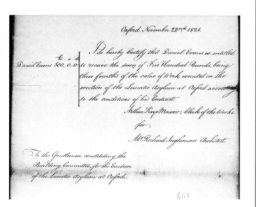

Payment authorisation for work executed at the Asylum

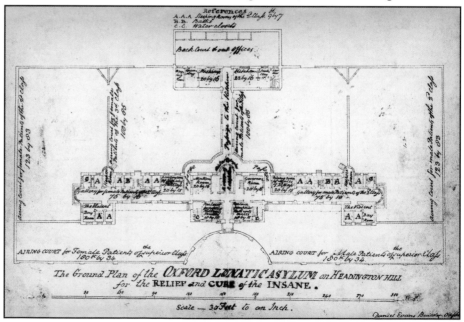

Evans' plan for the Radcliffe Asylum on Headington Hill

build the north wing, if so desired, within two years for a further £1,927. The foundation stone was laid by the Bishop of Oxford on 27 August 1821 and on this occasion no less than twenty-four loaves of bread, thirty-one pounds of cheese, a barrel of beer and a quantity of pipes and tobacco were supplied to Evans' workmen, the whole costing £5. 9s 5d.

A Clerk of Works, resident on the site, was appointed to supervise the building, subject to the architect's control. Stage payments were made to Evans as the work proceeded, the architect measuring up the work done and making out a certificate; one of £500 authorised in November 1821 was described as 'more than he was entitled to at the time.' The building was faced with Bath stone, with brick inside walls. Flooring and roofing were in Memel timber, windows, doors and shutters were of fir. The roof was covered with the best Cumberland slate; lead was used on cornices and to form gutters; windows were glazed with crown glass; ceilings and walls had three coats of plaster and were whitewashed.

At one stage Evans had to reassure the Committee of Management that the mortar on walls was made up of one third fresh burnt lime and two thirds of road drift sand, the same materials and proportions that were used on any Government works. Local Headington stone was used for court and boundary walls. While Evans was the contractor, he sub-contracted much of the work, probably doing the bricklaying and masonry with his own people; plumbing and glazing, slating, painting, blacksmith's work were clearly sub-contracted, some to tradesmen from Southwell possibly recommended by the architect and some to craftsmen from Northampton and Leicester, probably known to

Drawing by Evans of Chiselhampton House, Oxon. Alteration, extension and new portico, 1820

Evans carried out alterations to Merton College Chapel in 1823 (Oxford Almanack 1830)

Evans from his earlier work there. Evans received £8,246 on completion of the contract.

The building in late Georgian style was completed 'with relatively few mishaps', according to contemporary report. It is now hidden by a large extension built in 1877. The design was clearly ahead of its time for the care of the mentally ill, the galleries and corridors being built with regard to comfort and cheerfulness. Opened in July 1826 with thirty-nine patients, the Asylum, which charged 2 to 4 guineas per week according to the apartments occupied and attendance required, was clearly intended for the well-to-do. Evans was not engaged to provide a second wing and in 1830 another builder was adding store rooms.

Evans success in Oxford must have encouraged him to move from London where the building trade at the time, although not without opportunities, was

Evans designed and built the fine Georgian Rectory at Nuneham Courtenay in 1824

crowded and intensely competitive. With his reputation established, Evans was living in St. Mary Magdalen parish, close to the centre of Oxford, in 1823. He now enjoyed a prolific period. In 1824 he was engaged both to design and build the Rectory at Nuneham Courtenay, 7 miles from Oxford. Describing him as a 'skilful and experienced surveyor', the Rector employed Evans to report on the condition of the damp and inconvenient old Rectory and prepare a plan, specification and estimate for a new building. The Bishop approved and commissioners were appointed to select a builder. Evans described himself as being 'accustomed to survey and value and to superintend the building and repair of houses and buildings of all descriptions and also to value building materials.' His bond for £2,000 - presumably showing part of his assets - was duly sworn in Oxford, and he received the contract. The costs of the Rectory were met by a mortgage of £810 against glebe, tithe rents and other emoluments of the Rector.

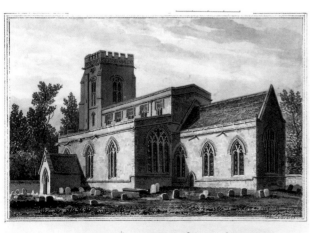

South East View of Great Tew Church, Oxfordshire

Two years later, in 1826, Evans undertook the refurbishment of Great Tew church to the designs of Thomas Rickman, the well known church architect, and at the time one of the busiest architects in England. Rickman had been commissioned by Matthew Robinson Boulton who had recently acquired the Great Tew estate. Here Evans' contract for the repairs was £1,245. Rickman, the architect, fell out with his clients in a dispute which involved both Evans and the Clerk of Works, the latter being the architect's site representative. Clearly Boulton and the churchwardens were not happy with some of the changes to the interior of the church which modified its

Oxford 10th March 1827

To Mr Barlow
Churchwarden of Gt Yew

Sir) I have taken the liberty of writing to you, to request you will send me word when I am to receive my Ballance for the Works done at Gt Yew Church which is as per Certificate for the the Church Acct £720.2.8 and which I sent to Mr Fulljames on Monday the 26th of February last but not receiving any Answere I sent again to him on Tuesday last but have not yet Received any Answere, I should not have written now but you Know my Agreement states that I am to Receive my Ballance on my Certificate being signed by the Architects. your Answere will much oblige Sir.

Yours Respectfully
Daniel Evans

Great Tew 10 mo/Octr/19 1826

To the Church Wardens of Great & Little Tew

We hereby certify that Mr Evans the Contractor for the repairs of the Church has now covered in the whole of the Roofs & is therefore entitled under his Contract to a Payment of Six Hundred twenty two Pounds twelve Shillings & Six pence

Witness our Hand
Rickman & Hutchinson
Architects

style and character. Probably because of this dispute Evans had difficulty in being paid the balance of his contract in March 1827.

Within Oxford, and working for the first time with the local architect, H.J. Underwood, Evans was employed to carry out repairs to the chancel, spire and roof of St. Aldate's church, carrying on with the remodelling of its interior in 1832. Meanwhile, a new college connection began at Pembroke in 1829 when Evans was awarded the contract to reface in Bath stone the seventeenth century Old Quad, within and without, and raise the tower by

Old Quad, Pembroke College: refaced in the Gothic style and tower raised by a storey - 1829-30

Broad Street front, Exeter College. Evans' range to the east 1833-34. His partner and successor, Joshua Symm built the entrance tower and range to the west 1854-56

Opposite page:
34-36 St. Giles', substantial town houses designed and built by Evans in 1828. He himself lived in 34, as did his son-in-law, Joshua Symm, subsequently.

The Ordnance Survey map shows the gardens and stables to the rear and the Builder's Yard and Workshop with access to Little Clarendon Street, where some of Evans' and Symm's craftsmen were living at the time.

one storey in the Gothic style, apparently to his own design. The result attracted subsequent criticism, being variously described as 'a great pity', 'a misguided effort.' Evans' contract was for £2,898. The east side of the Quad initially escaped, to be finished in 1838 in the same style at a cost of £5,270.

Further work, and the beginning of an important connection, followed in 1833/34 when Evans built the new east range at Exeter College's Broad Street front, also to the designs of H.J. Underwood. This contract was for £3,574 and the expenses of a supper for workmen were recorded at £10.9s, clearly a large group being employed on the project. The Broad Street front featured Gothic ornament, as did the refacing of the Turl Street front in Bath stone, also by Underwood in 1834-35, but the builder then used was another local firm, Plowmans. Meanwhile Evans continued to do repairs in the College over the following years; his successor Joshua Symm was to do some of his finest and most ambitious college building there later.

Evans, although primarily an institutional builder, became involved in the development of the Beaumont Street area in the late 1820s. As a speculation for himself he built Nos. 20-22 St. John Street and he may have built other houses on contract for investors. In 1828 successful and established as he then was, Evans designed and built three fine adjacent houses, Nos. 34-36 St. Giles', the one at no. 34 St. Giles' being for his own occupation, the

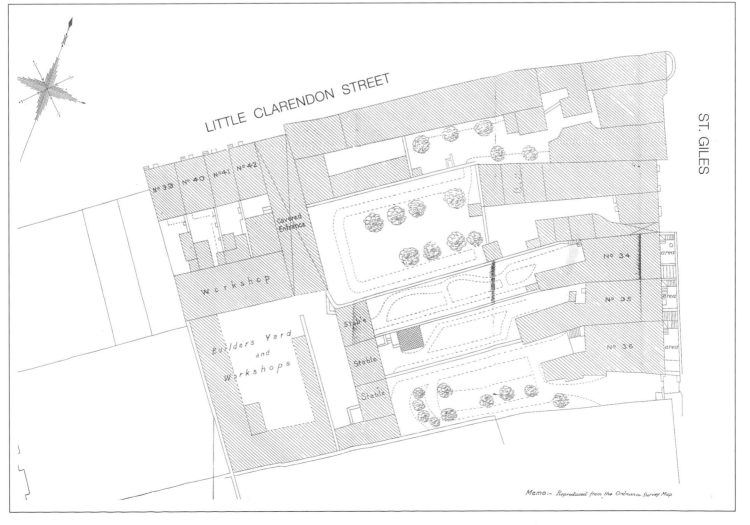

LITTLE CLARENDON STREET

ST. GILES

Nº 39 Nº 40 Nº 41 Nº 42

Covered Entrance

Workshop

Builders Yard and Workshops

Stable

Stable

Stable

Nº 34

Nº 35

Nº 36

area

area

area

Memo:- Reproduced from the Ordnance Survey Map

others being let. These were built on a ninety-nine year lease at a ground rent of £22 per annum. Handsome houses as they were, built on three floors with a large drawing room on the first floor and servants' quarters on the third, the address itself was prestigious and Evans' neighbours were successful tradesmen or retired gentlefolk. The property, leased from the Oxford surgeon John Bull (who also owned all the farmland, as it was then, between Rawlinson Road and South Parade), was L-shaped and reached to Little Clarendon Street at the back. Here Evans established his yard with convenient access to the garden of 34 St. Giles'. He would manage the building business from here, store materials, pay his workmen, and provide workshop space for carpenters and joiners, and stonemasons, as well as stabling for horses; he also dealt in timber, bricks and probably stone as a merchant from these Little Clarendon premises. Although now firmly established in Oxford, he still did projects outside, designing and building the Vicarage at Churcham in Gloucestershire in 1839.

Evans was seventy-one in 1840. He had no son and needed a successor.

Evans and Symm, the new Partnership, built the north side of Chapel Quad, Pembroke College, in 1844-45

Joshua Robinson Symm had joined him as a stonemason, sometime in the 1830s. Born in Allendale, Northumberland in 1809, he had no doubt migrated to Oxford in search of improved livelihood. Competent and diligent at his trade and as a manager of workmen, he became Evans' foreman. He was also a Methodist and the two men clearly established a relationship of respect and confidence. Symm married Evans' only daughter, Elizabeth, and the families were living together at 34 St. Giles' in 1841. Evans, regarding him as the person to carry his business forward, then admitted Symm to partnership. Thus the Directories of the 1840s. refer to 'Evans and Symm' as builders. As an indication of their standing they were probably one of the first customers of the London and County Bank (later part of National Westminster) when it opened a branch in Oxford High Street in 1843.

It was this enterprise, Evans and Symm, which was engaged to extend the buildings of Pembroke College in 1844-46. Their accepted tender was for £5,287 to build the north side of the second or garden quadrangle of the College to the architectural plans of Charles Hayward of Exeter, nephew and pupil of Sir Charles Barry. These New Buildings, provided a new Senior Common Room and Bursary and a range of rooms for fellows and undergraduates. The College then decided to build a new Hall at right angles to the New Buildings with Hayward again being the architect. Evans and Symm lost the tender to a London builder. Pevsner describes the Quad as a whole as 'spacious and attractive all round in the variety of its features.'

The buildings at Pembroke were the last major work to be constructed by Daniel Evans. He died in November 1846, aged seventy-seven, and, with his wife, was buried in the graveyard behind the Methodist Chapel he had built. He was a gifted and energetic man who won the confidence of important patrons and leading architects of the day, creating a significant enterprise for the trade in which he engaged. He made his mark, accordingly, on the buildings of the University and established the strong association which was to continue under his successors.

The Rev.d the Rector & Fellows

of Exeter College

Gentlemen

The Cost of the new Gates in Broad
Street made in English Oak to the design furnished
will be £140 . 0 . 0
The above sum does not however include Iron work
and Fastenings and fixing the same

_____

The additional story to wood Building
in Turl Street between Exeter College and Mr Parker.
& Couse will be £140 . 0 . 0

I am Gentlemen,
yours very Respectfully

9th March 1859

CHAPTER

GOTHIC REVIVAL: 1846-1887
JOSHUA ROBINSON SYMM

Following the death of Daniel Evans, the business passed to Joshua Symm. It was to trade under his name and control until, with increasing age, Symm brought his principal colleagues into partnership in 1874, but he remained actively involved until shortly before his death in 1887. The period of Symm's leadership was the high period when the business carried out some of its most significant work in Oxford.

Much of Symm's greatest work was carried out in association with the distinguished architect Sir Gilbert Scott in two colleges, Exeter and Christ Church, but also at University College. Unquestionably the relationship was a harmonious one, with the architect confident that the Oxford builder would execute his plans and designs faithfully with sensitive and skilled workmanship and without creating any problems of delay or pricing. The relationship with Scott apart, Symm and his associates clearly won the confidence of a number of colleges as a reliable builder who could carry out any kind of college work from mundane repairs, introduction of new facilities to do with sanitation and comfort, enlargement, refurbishment and restoration, or entirely new buildings all to the highest standard, and sensitive to the heritage of fine and unique architecture. Symm, of all the Oxford builders, will take care of it, became the accepted proposition.

The work at Exeter College, after Christ Church, one of the larger colleges at the time, was the first major college enterprise. Evans had built the Broad Street front east of the tower in 1833 and the firm continued to do repair work over the following years. Now in 1854, Symm was contracted to extend the Broad Street front westward providing eighteen sets of rooms, and build a tower and a gateway at a cost of £4,587. He seems then to have become the regular College builder; a special account book for 1856-89 survives showing a stream of small building and repair jobs over the years; indeed there would be few months when Symm's workmen were not engaged in one task or another at Exeter, fixing a window, replacing a fireplace, strengthening a wall. But there were the more memorable larger tasks. In 1856 the College took the decision to build a new Chapel, on the north side of the Front Quad, replacing the old Chapel which was too small to meet the needs of compulsory attendance, and had allegedly become dangerous;

Work in progress at Prideaux's Building, Exeter College 1850s

43

it was described as 'damp, dark, with a detestable stove which gave out no heat and volumes of fetid smoke.' A competition was held and from the designs submitted those of George Gilbert Scott were accepted. Scott said of his design that it was 'in the style which prevailed on or about the original foundation of the College (1314), the period of highest perfection attained by Gothic architecture.'

Symm contracted to build the new Chapel for £7,900, although in the end he received £11,591 when the work was completed. So large a difference was not unusual in building projects at this time, invariably the result of changes in concept, materials or features agreed between architect and client. Members of the College, both past and present, met most of the cost; the Rector and almost all members of the foundation gave a year's income. The completed building was consecrated by Samuel Wilberforce, Bishop of Oxford, on 18th October 1859. After a sermon by the College Visitor, 300 guests sat down to a sumptuous luncheon. Symm's workmen were entertained subsequently to the customary 'dinner of a substantial character, washed down by a plentiful supply of good College ale, followed by pipes and tobacco and, to diversify the proceedings, songs and toasts.'

Exeter College Chapel is a monument to the Gothic revival, one of its most characteristic productions. The shape and style owes much to the inspiration of the Ste. Chapelle in Paris. Distinguished Victorian artists like Burne-Jones and William Morris (himself an undergraduate of Exeter, 1852-55) made their

A monument to the Gothic revival; Exeter College Chapel, designed by Sir Gilbert Scott and built by Joshua Symm, 1857-59. The photographs show the Chapel under construction and the Chapel today

contribution subsequently. Building craftsmen marvelled at the ornate, beautiful soaring building with its vast windows, set between buttresses, preparing the visitor for 'the internal effect of the stone-ribbed vault, screen and organ-loft, the wooden canopied stalls and the stained glass'. The stone and wood carving both outside and in the interior was remarkable. Some complained of uneven workmanship and of a building out of proportion to the rest of the Quad and somewhat overpowering it. Some just regretted the replacement of the old, the destructive spirit as they termed it, that was abroad in Oxford, in Exeter, Balliol, Jesus and elsewhere.

To rebuild the Chapel with additional length to the old building which preceded it, the old Rector's Lodgings had to be demolished. To Scott's designs, Symm built new Rector's Lodgings in 1856-57. Scott had also designed, in Gothic Revival style, a new Library, attractively sited in the College garden for which Symm again was the builder in 1856. Over this period, say 1854-1859, Symm carried out building work amounting to over £24,000, a huge undertaking at the time. Symm was to do further work on the Chapel in the 1870s, replacing the altar steps and placing sculptures of St. John, St. Andrew and other saints, executed by Farmer and Brindley of London, in niches on the Chapel wall. Exeter College has continued to use Symm and Company for various building and restoration works to the present day.

Symm's association with Christ Church, much the largest of the colleges, began in the 1860s. As elsewhere in the University, Christ Church needed more undergraduate accommodation to supplement that in The Great Quadrangle (Tom Quad) and Peckwater Quadrangle. A decision was made

As part of extensive work at Exeter College, Symm built a new Rector's Lodgings. The Reverend of an Oxford college, unlike the fellows, was married and his lodgings would accommodate a large family, servants and visitors

opposite page:
Exeter Chapel interior

Exeter College: Library, 1856

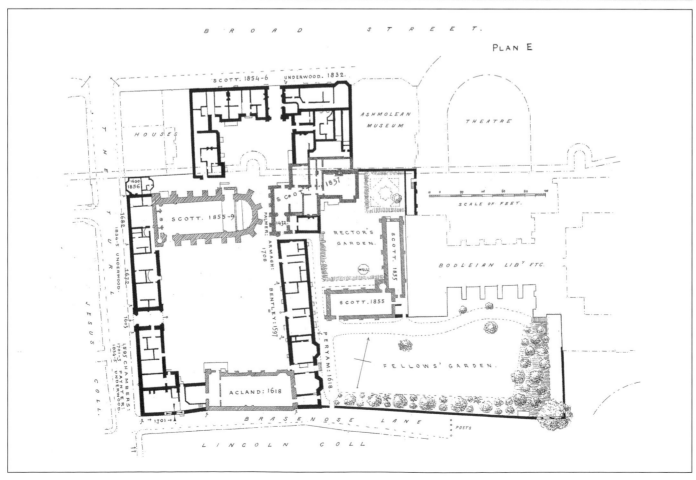

to build a range of new rooms fronting Christ Church Meadow; following a competition the designs of a Dublin architect T. N. Deane were accepted and contracts placed with J.R. Symm to construct what became Meadow Buildings, providing fifty-one sets of rooms, in 1863. A large project, the new building was completed at a cost of over £22,000 in 1866. Critics were not impressed, pseudo Venetian Gothic, big and heavy, joyless and dull, as it was described, 'a monument to Ruskin and his architectural doctrine'.

Meadow Buildings had been the initiative of Dean Liddell, famous not merely as head of the College (1855-91), but also as father of Alice, the friend of the Revd. Charles Dodgson (Lewis Carroll) and the inspiration of *'Alice in Wonderland'*. Liddell was the driving force behind all the building work that was to take place at Christ Church in the following period. Thus he involved Sir Gilbert Scott with the restoration of Christ Church Cathedral between 1870 and 1876. Symm was the chosen builder, thus continuing the close association formed at Exeter a decade earlier. The restoration was a major work which brought the Cathedral in all essential points to its present condition. The whole project cost £24,000, (£1.5 million in today's money). New windows, a large main entrance from Tom Quad, rebuilding of the 17th century south porch and doorway in the cloisters and the fine ribbed vault north of the Chapter House were important parts. The whole of the east end was rebuilt with a magnificent rose window to correspond with the surrounding Norman architecture. Coats of whitewash were cleaned off from the walls and the stonework restored. Old stone floors in the Nave and Choir were

Meadow front of Chaplains' Buildings, Christ Church. Chaplains' Quadrangle was rebuilt after a fire in 1669 and together with Fell's Building was taken down to make way for Meadow Buildings (Oxford Almanack 1864)

Meadow Buildings, Christ Church, completed by Symm in 1866. This was his first large project for the College

taken up and replaced with black and white marble. London specialists did the wood carving and the stained glass, but Symm's joiners made the impressive new stalls and seating for the Nave and Choir, all from selected walnut, in what had become the Home Yard at Little Clarendon Street. During the restoration the bells from the central tower were removed. Scott built a temporary wooden belfry, ridiculed at time as the 'meat-safe' or 'tea-chest', above the south-east corner of Tom Quad and re-hung the bells in it.

opposite page:
Symm worked with Sir Gilbert Scott on the alteration and restoration of Christ Church Cathedral in the 1870s

Symm was commissioned to carry out a major restoration of Tom Quad in the period 1874-80. At one stage it was contemplated to build cloisters all round the Quad and an estimate was prepared. Such a scheme was costly as well as controversial and in the event the 17th century buildings round Tom Quad were extensively refaced with Doulton stone, the terrace was lowered, many of the rooms were enlarged and battlements replaced the balustrades, with pinnacles to the Hall. Dean Liddell who commissioned the work, commented: 'the crumbling surface of the soft oolite stone...long disintegrated by rain and frost, was renewed with a harder stone'; he refers to 'an almost over-conscientious reproduction of Wolsey's unfinished project.'

Christ Church: before Wolsey Tower was built

The old belfry tower over the grand staircase to the Great Hall had been incomplete since Wolsey's day. In 1873 the Dean and Senior Students called for designs for a new proper belfry. They excluded Scott from the competition although at the last minute he submitted designs along with other distinguished architects of the period, including Basil Champneys and

Wolsey Tower,
(Oxford Almanack, 1881)

T.G. Jackson. Bodley and Garner won the competition with plans to construct an elaborate Gothic fantasy, but in the end almost every detail of the design was thrashed out, stage by stage, with the College committee charged with supervision of the task. The result, Wolsey Tower, built by Symm between 1876 and 1879, is simply a screen hiding the 'meat-safe'; it 'sits ponderously in the south-east corner of Tom Quad, a monument to the vacillation of a Governing Body which, having chosen a grand design, did not have the courage to carry it out.'*
Again working to the designs of Bodley and

* Howard Colvin, *Unbuilt Oxford* (1983), p140.

When Symm installed new drains, as at Christ Church, he left his own manhole cover

Symm's invoice for sanitary work at Christ Church in 1891

Garner, now the favoured college architects, Symm also built the counterpart to Wolsey Tower, the upper part of the so-called Fell Tower to the north-east of the Quad. This programme of major work at Christ Church was completed in 1880 with the restoration of the Chapter House of the Cathedral and with work on the Picture Gallery and Library.

Throughout this decade of the 1870s the Oxford builder had proved his competence to carry out structural repairs and new work to the treasured historic buildings of the College, not merely sensitively but consistent with the character of the original and with a minimum of disruption to the life and work of the institution. Thomas Hardy, himself the son of a stonemason, clearly had Symm's work at Christ Church in mind when he wrote *Jude the Obscure*. In the novel Jude became a mason at a stoneyard said to be based on Symm's Oxford stone works. He was working at the fictional Cardinal College, Christminster, restoring decaying college buildings. Hardy describes the yard as 'a little centre of regeneration' where 'with keen edges and smooth curves, were forms in the exact likeness of those...abraded and time-eaten on the walls.' Hardy describes 'the new traceries, mullions, transoms, shafts, pinnacles, and battlements standing on the bankers half-worked, or waiting to be removed. They were marked by precision, mathematical straightness, smoothness, exactitude', ready to replace in the old walls 'the broken lines of the original idea.' Hardy, through Jude, concluded 'that here in the stoneyard was a centre of effort as worthy as that dignified by the name of scholarly study within the noblest of colleges.'

One may suppose the Governing Body, if not sharing Hardy's latter sentiments, were pleased with the work of their builder. They continued to employ Symm along with Wyatt, another college builder, who did many mundane jobs, altering undergraduate rooms or changing Canon's lodgings, for example. In 1881 Symm upgraded the system of drainage throughout the College 'on the latest sanitary principles', installing water-closets and separating rainwater drains from the sewers. In 1883 three Lecture Rooms were created on the ground floor of the Old Library, and the stone windows of the Hall restored. Not everything was straightforward. In 1888 Symm's successors were again at work on the drains rousing complaints from Revd. Charles Dodgson, then

Curator of the Senior Common Room, regarding 'evil odours' in the Common Room, and 'a stifling and noxious atmosphere which is unendurable'; if builders stirred up these problems they also put them right. Symm and Company's next large project at the College was to be in the 1900s when the firm restored the St. Aldate's front and Tom Tower. Christ Church was to remain a regular major client to the present day.

Whilst Exeter and Christ Church were two of the main clients of Joshua Symm during the third quarter of the century the firm was also active at University College, building the new Library, the Buttery and altering and restoring the Chapel, all for architect Sir Gilbert Scott over the period 1859-63. Further work was to follow here at intervals to the present day. He worked for other colleges too, namely All Souls where he refaced the Catte Street frontage around 1850. But it is clear that other builders participated in the large amount of college building that took place in Oxford in the main Symm period, that is the third quarter of the century. Thus to quote some examples, much of the work at Balliol, associated with the architects Butterfield and Waterhouse, was carried out by the London builder W.M. Brass. At Merton,

Library interior

Library, University College (Oxford Almanack 1862)

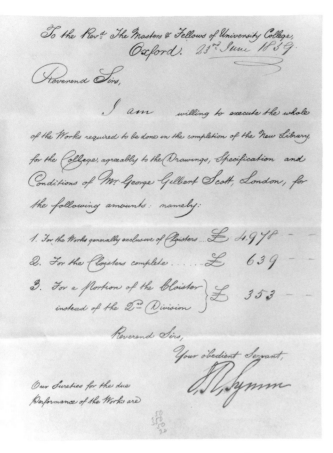

J.R. Symm's estimate for the new Library, University College, 1859

Butterfield was also the architect for the Grove Buildings (1864) and Gilbert Scott became involved with remodelling the Hall in 1872-74; here London builders were also engaged. Gilbert Scott was employed at New College to make modifications to the Hall (1865), and especially on the Holywell Buildings in 1872 and in 1877 restoration of the Chapel: most of this work was carried out by builders from outside Oxford, although the College was employing Symm on its Choristers' School in 1874.

St. John's was another college which substantially increased its undergraduate accommodation after 1850, also involving Gilbert Scott. Jesus College employed the architect J.C. Buckler for thirty years after 1852. Most of the work was restoration and renovation and modest enlargement and went to the Oxford builder Wyatt. Wyatt also seems to have been busy at Wadham in the period, in laying piped water throughout, hot water heating in the Chapel and Library, and improving the Lodgings. The same builder carried out much of the mundane work at Worcester during this period. And of course, the largest college building project of this period, namely Keble College, over the years 1868-1882, went to outside builders, Franklin of Deddington and Parnell and Sons of Rugby.

The third quarter of the century also saw significant new university as distinct from college building. The Ashmolean Museum and Taylor Institution was built by Baker of Lambeth in the 1840s. The University Museum, the work of Sir Thomas Deane and Benjamin Woodward, was started in 1854 and attracted much attention, the builder being the London firm Lucas Brothers. But the major University buildings were to come later in the century.

However it was in 1868 that Symm was given the major task of building the first purpose-designed physics laboratory in the country, which was to become known as the Clarendon Laboratory. Sir Thomas Deane was the architect. An extract from the late A.J. Croft's *Oxford's Clarendon Laboratory,* written in 1985, but not published, throws light upon a builder's relations with a University client at the time:

> Curiously, there was no transfer of money from the Clarendon Trustees to the University - the administrative arrangements of the building work were handled by the Trustees and their solicitors in London, Boodle and Partington of Berkeley Square, and the University solicitors, Morrell and Hawkins in Oxford.
>
> The eight tenders were opened on 10 July 1868 in the house of the Secretary of the Trustees, Sir William Heathcote, in the presence of Sir Thomas Deane and another anonymous person. The lowest, that of

Messrs. Symm, still in business in Oxford - was found to be £1,200 in excess of the available funds and Deane was asked to amend his proposals in consultation with Professor Clifton. This evidently went smoothly because by 31 August the contractors raised two objections which threatened the Trustees with 'great additional expense'. They were told 'either give up the contract or withdraw'. The progress of the building can be gauged by the transfers of cash from the deposit account at the London and Westminster Bank: £1,200 in January 1869,

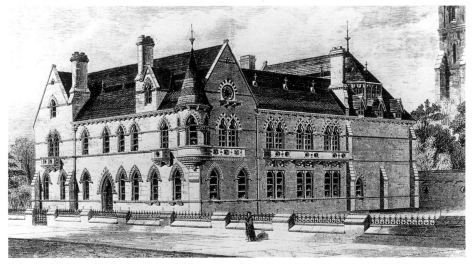

The Clarendon Laboratory, 1868-70 - a contemporary engraving

far left:
Switchboard, believed to be one of the first of its kind.

left:
Engine Room

The Clarendon Laboratory

The Clarendon Laboratory: floor plan.

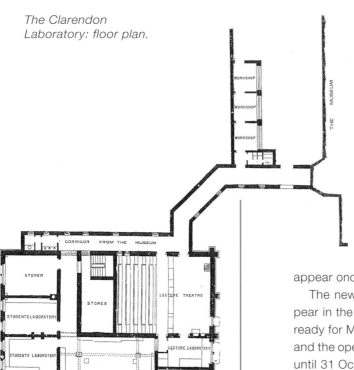

£1,600 in June, £1,600 in August, £1,500 in March 1870, £1,600 in June and finally £1,800 in March 1871, leaving £600 on deposit. Each payment to the Architect, contractors and Clerk of Works involved this chain: Symm - Deane - Morrell and Hawkins - Boodle and Partington - Duke of Marlborough - Boodle and Partington - Earl of Caernarvon - Boodle and Partington - London and Westminster Bank - Morrell and Hawkins - Symm, the traditional 6s. 8d being the solicitors' fee each time. There was also much exchanging of paper when sums were moved from the deposit to the current or 'drawing' account.

There was an exchange of letters between Clifton and Lord Caernarvon from early in 1871 which has perished in a purge at Boodle and Partington of 1951. These must have concerned the spending of the balance on what appear once in the Bill Book as fittings.

The new 'Physical Laboratory' - its eponymous title does not appear in the *University Gazette* until October 1873 - was to have been ready for Michaelmas 1870 but then as now building projects ran late and the opening of the Professor's lecture course had to be postponed until 31 October.

A final meeting of the Clarendon Trustees was arranged for 27 July 1872 at 10 Downing Street but the other Trustees failed to turn up and arrangements were made to wind up the Trust by correspondence.

As the remaining balance dwindled the correspondence between Professor Clifton and Lord Caernarvon became lengthier and more frequent and there were journeys to Oxford by members of Boodle and Partington staff about the details of the inscription on vellum* by a Mr Wyatt, and of the carved lintel, part of which is preserved. Finally, the Trustees' account was closed in October 1874. (This lintel reads '1872' but it is certain that the new building came into use late in 1870.)

Meanwhile in the town of Oxford, Symm was again involved at St. Aldate's church in the work carried out in 1874 by the Victorian restorer, J.T. Christopher. The firm rebuilt the tower and spire at this time (It was to return to St. Aldate's again in the 1960s). Outside Oxford, Symm was employed in 1855 to extend Shotover House near Wheatley, the original 18th century building being the work of William Townesend, the great Oxford master builder of the time. This was a sensitive commission which subsequent owners of Shotover acknowledge was carried out with great skill.

Three other areas of work associated with Joshua Symm merit mention. His firm participated, if only modestly, in the extensive development of North Oxford after 1860. He built three villas on Banbury Road, the one at 64 Banbury Road, designed by E.G. Bruton (a pupil of Underwood) being a particularly fine example of the graciousness and dignity to which successful

Shotover House

opposite page:
No. 64 Banbury Road, Oxford, built for the corn dealer John Weaving, 1873

* Visible on the first floor of the Lindemann Building, Clarendon Laboratory

Victorians aspired in their family homes. There were also two villas on South Parks Road and No. 8 Kingston Road, designed by Thomas Axtell for Mr. Pauling and built in 1879. But generally, Joshua Symm steered clear of speculative house-building in North Oxford and elsewhere in the town, and the same was largely true of his successors.

More typically in 1873 he was engaged to build the Chapel at St. Edward's School which had recently moved from central Oxford to a site in Summertown. Financed entirely by donations from parents, Symm contracted to build the Chapel for £5,000, completing the project in 1876. The opening, despite pouring rain, seems to have been a lively affair, with a choir singing appropriate psalms from the scaffolding, an Old Boys match, a band concert and a fireworks display. Thirty-five of Symm's workmen enjoyed the customary 'sumptuous repast' which marked these completions. Subsequently, in 1879, Symm was building the Entrance Lodge as well as accommodation for the staff.

Throughout his life in Oxford Joshua Symm had been closely involved with the Methodist Chapel. In 1851 he became Superintendent of its Sunday School. During lean years for the Methodists, he had carried out repairs or alterations to the buildings without pressing for payment. In 1871, with Methodism flourishing in the city, it was decided to build a new larger chapel in New Inn Hall Street, in front of the old. Symm was the builder and with others laid a foundation stone, no doubt contributing to the cost. The new chapel, built to a conventional gothic style, had a spacious grandeur and reflected craftsmanship to a high standard, not least in the fine carved capitals of the pillars. A feature was the fine stained glass windows including one given by Symm in 1879 in memory of his daughter and only child, Hannah, who died in 1875. When the chapel was opened on 11 October 1878, collections at the ceremony amounted to the considerable sum of £340. Meanwhile the trustees began a new programme with Symm to convert the old chapel into classrooms and a lecture room. The total amount raised for building the new chapel and converting the old building

Entrance Lodge, St. Edward's School

opposite page:
The Chapel, St. Edward's School

Symm was closely associated with the Methodist cause in Oxford and built a further chapel in 1878

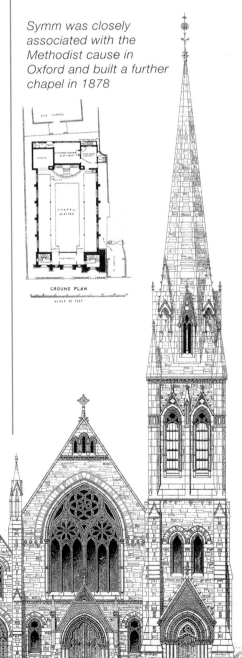

was £11,331 while £13,999 was spent on the two projects, large sums but not untypical of the amount that Victorians were spending on new churches and chapels at this period.

Symm was a cautious conservative employer, frugal and careful in his practices. Richard Evans, who was apprenticed to the firm in 1864, recalls a master who had an eagle eye for waste in any form; as an example Evans recalled Symm spotting nails on the ground and saying 'Man, pick them up, it's no use sowing them, they will not grow.' During this period, the 1860s and 1870s, the hours of work remained fifty eight and a half for the normal week, from 6 a.m. to 5.30 p.m. through the week with the day ending at 4 p.m. on Saturday; breakfast and dinner took one and a half hours. Starting so early in the morning not least when the job was far from home, the men would typically send out for ale at breakfast, occasionally using a spotlessly clean shovel to fry eggs over a fire; dinner would follow the same kind of practice. Symm was always present when his men were paid on Saturday afternoons. Irrespective of where they were working the men were paid at the Home Yard in Little Clarendon Street, each man being called into the office where the Chief Clerk would count his money, put it into a bowl when Mr. Symm would check it and hand it to the man. This was a slow business, especially when Symm demanded an account of the work.

But Joshua Symm was growing old. He had a successful business but no sons to succeed him. In a relationship which paralleled that between himself and Daniel Evans over 30 years earlier, he had given increasing responsibility to one of his employees, Thomas Axtell, a skilled, indeed gifted, stonemason, already General Foreman and supervisor of the important work at Christ

Thomas Axtell's drawing of the Wren Screen in the Chapel, Merton College

opposite page:
The Tower of Five Orders, Schools Quad, Bodleian Library, following stone restoration, 1870s/80s

Church. Axtell, born in 1826, was one of a family of active masons in Oxford and elsewhere: he was related to the Axtell's who carried on a monumental and general masons business in Oxford as W.H. Axtell, and to the Axtell who had gone into partnership with a Butcher as Butcher and Axtell, masons and sculptors, in Camberwell. Thomas Axtell had joined Symm in 1848. In 1871 he was living with his wife and seven children (and a maid) at 8, Commercial Road in St. Ebbe's, describing himself as a master mason and grocer: his wife probably augmented his income by running a small shop. Symm had other trusted associates, Thomas Howard, for many years the Chief Clerk, and Benjamin Hart, foreman of joiners. However conservatively, given the length of their association, Joshua Symm admitted them all to partnership in 1874, the new concern continuing to trade as J.R. Symm and Company.

The Partnership capital at the outset was £1,000, divided into sixteen shares, Symm holding six, Howard four and Axtell and Hart three each. Interest on the capital was to be paid at the usual rate of 5 per cent before profit was struck. The new business took over materials and tools at Symm's yards, valued at £1,659 and this sum was regarded as a debt due to Symm; he retained ownership of the Little Clarendon Street yard (no. 43) and received a rent of £70 per annum. Provided the balance remaining at the bank was greater than £150, and the 'floating' capital was not less than £1,000, the Partners were to take annual salaries at £275 in the case of Symm, £130 for Howard, and £110 for Axtell and Hart. These were modest enough sums but would be augmented by interest on their capital and by drawings from annual profits as these were made. While Joshua Symm was required only to devote so much time as he pleased to the business the other Partners committed themselves to faithful and diligent service, and not to engage in any calling, business, or undertaking which might conflict. Interestingly the Partners were not to take any apprentice or hire or dismiss any 'clerk, workman or servant' without the consent of Joshua Symm.

While he remained the senior Partner, one may suppose that Symm played a diminishing role. Increasingly the energy and initiative of the new business would be that of the younger Partners and, it seems, Thomas Axtell in particular. Thus Symm and Co. became much more active in the late 1870s onwards: in part this reflected a surge in college and University building activity but it was also due to the enterprise of the new Partners.

A number of major University assignments were now undertaken, not least the restoration of the venerable Bodleian Library. Symm had been called in to examine the state of both roof and floors of the Old Reading Room; their report greatly alarmed the Curators, drawing attention to decayed timbers, displaced walls and serious fire risks. Work started in the Long Vacation of

1876, and continued over several years, each change to the historic structure, however carefully carried out, being the subject of anguished argument and controversy. The removal of fine oak bookcases, the original furnishing of Sir Thomas Bodley, and the decision whether or not to return them, for instance, brought much debate among the Curators. In the end they were put back, if only temporarily, although some had been knocked to pieces, probably on the suggestion of Benjamin Jowett, Master of Balliol. The Librarian, Coxe, could write in his diary, 'the dear old cases all up again' and a few days later, no doubt when the interior was completed and the disruption at an end, 'Dear old Bodley itself again and looking so nice.' Symm would have long experience in dealing with such sensitive clients.

Apart from the interior, external repairs were urgent; the stone facing of the Library was much weather-worn and broken, especially on windows, parapets, pinnacles and cornices; parts were in an extremely dangerous state, while extensive refacing of the walls and the tower was necessary. The architect T.G. Jackson (1835-1924) by now possibly Oxford's favourite, in part because he was a college fellow and a senior member of the University,

Schools Quad, Bodleian Library, following stone restoration, 1870s/80s

Indian Institute, view from Broad Street

Indian Institute: ceremonial stone-laying, 1883

directed the work of restoration, again of the most delicate and sensitive kind. Thus some of the great windows of the Library with sixteenth and seventeenth century Flemish and German stained glass had to be reglazed or renewed; much of the glass was broken when taken out for reglazing and had to be put together again; in all fifty four windows had to be restored with new sills, jambs and mullions and lead glazing made good. There were twenty new pinnacles. Jackson had no confidence in the local material, Headington or Taynton stone from the Windrush valley, which had been used in the old building. He wanted the more durable Clipsham stone from Rutland. Its delivered price was the same but its hardness made it more costly to work. Jackson eventually overcame the Curator's resistance on this account and Clipsham was used in refacing, one of the first uses of what was to become the most preferred stone for Oxford buildings for the next hundred years.

Symm began the external restoration in 1878 and, as contract succeeded contract, the work went on until 1884. The London specialist McCulloch did much of the fine stone carving. Throughout this period the Bodleian precincts reverberated with the screech of stone saws. When completed the University had spent £26,440. However well executed the result was controversial. As the historian of the Bodleian commented, 'Viewed from neighbouring roofs the result is magnificent - but the usual view-point is from the ground and not so happy,' given the sharp contrasts between light coloured Clipsham above and the older darker rougher Headington below with an unsightly patchwork in the middle. The aged John Ruskin, it was said, was so offended by the restored Bodleian, that he did his best to avoid passing it!

Another noteworthy new Oxford building at this time was the flamboyant Indian Institute, at the end of Broad Street, where Symm built the first stage between 1882 and 1884 to Basil Champneys' design, but Parnell of Rugby won the contract for the southern half, completed in 1896. Symm missed out on the work on the Oxford Union building, carried out between 1872 and 1878 by local builders such as Wyatt and outsiders like Parnell. Another large and prestigious project was the Examination Schools in the High Street, a building made necessary because of the increasing number of candidates presenting themselves for examination; previously examinations had been held in the Bodleian, the Sheldonian Theatre or even the Clarendon Building. After a major competition, the designs of T.G Jackson were accepted but Symm was unsuccessful in the tender and the building contract went to Estcourt of Gloucester, the work taking place between 1877 and 1881; the other early use of Clipsham stone. Symm did, however, build other central University facilities at this time, the University Observatory extension in 1877-78, laboratories for Inorganic Chemistry, 1877-79, and Physiology, 1884-85, and the Pitt Rivers Museum in 1885-86; for these science buildings Symm again worked with the architect T.N. Deane. Another important client in 1886 was the Clarendon Press which enlarged its buildings at the time. The Department of Human Anatomy, designed by H.W. Moore, then followed, adjoining the east end of the Pitt Rivers Museum, in 1892-93.

Finally new college work came on the scene, notably again at University

Inorganic Chemistry Laboratory, 1877-79

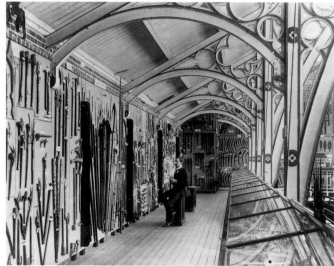

Pitt Rivers Museum, 1885-86

from 1877, including the conversion of the old Master's House into undergraduate rooms in 1879, followed by an ongoing programme of restoration and refacing that continued into the 20th century. At Brasenose in 1882-83 Knowles seems to have succeeded Wyatt as the main College builder; but Symm won the contract for the west and north sides of the new South Quad. They continued their association with T.G. Jackson whose exuberant style was accepted for the large extension of accommodation forming the start of the new Quad which was completed in 1889 with the range and gateway fronting the High Street. At the new Wycliffe Hall, with the architects Wilkinson and Moore, Symm built a large extension in 1881

University College: plan by J.R. Symm, signed TA (Thomas Axtell) and dated 1875

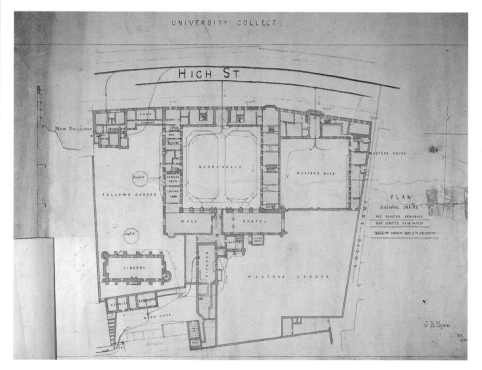

incorporating eleven sets of undergraduate rooms and a huge lecture room. Subsequently the firm carried out other major works here, including the Chapel in 1896. St. John's was another important client with Symm beginning to build a new Quad in 1880, with Gilbert Scott's son, George Gilbert Junior as the architect

Within the City of Oxford itself, the Symm Partnership was also seeking more general public and commercial work. In 1871 it had built one of the earliest schools, at Paradise Square in St. Ebbe's, to the design of Basil Champneys; this was an extension of an earlier school, the first church school in Oxford, founded by Champneys' father when he had been in charge of St. Ebbe's parish forty years before. Symm was to build the new Post Office in 1878-79, a large contract worth over £10,000. Symm built the charitable

Oxford High School for Girls, 1879

Hospital for Incurables in Cowley St. John, at the time a growing suburb, and between 1871 and 1883 was also involved in the building enlargement or restoration of several Oxford churches, notably the restoration of the University Church of St. Mary in High Street, St. Giles' Church, and the Church of St. Mary and St. John in Cowley Road. In Joshua Symm's later years there was involvement in commercial building; shops, banks, offices, hotels in the emerging town centre, and a further two houses along the Woodstock Road, numbers 137 and 139, as well as two large houses on South Parks Road, numbers 7 and 9.

Outside Oxford, a more characteristic contract for Symm was the extension of the fine Georgian villa, Woodperry, near Stanton St. John, which had been built by William Townesend the elder between 1728 and 1731, partly in the Palladian style, partly Baroque. It was too small for the new owner, John Thomson, a successful banker, and the architect Frederick Codd was commissioned to design north and south wings to the original house. Symm was chosen in the subsequent competition although his estimate, at £4,227, was the second highest of the four tenders submitted. The owner negotiated a reduction of £150 but in the end Symm received £4,500.

Woodperry House: wings added, 1880

What was described as 'sympathetic additions to the original house' were completed in 1880, the new wings being built in Bath stone and the work being extended to the stables and estate cottages. Symm incorporated a fine 18th century plaster moulding, found in a builder's yard, in the new drawing room. (Interestingly, in 1996, Symm was appointed to carry out major refurbishment and restoration of the same property for its new owner.)

All this busy activity was reflected in increased staff and greater profitability. The business now occupied three yards: the Home Yard with joinery workshops at Little Clarendon Street and stoneyard with masons' workshops at Cromwell Street in St. Ebbe's, close to Christ Church; there was also a third small yard and office in Brewer Street serving Christ Church and that district. At the Census of 1881 Joshua Symm was recorded as employing 155 people. As a building employer his normal workforce was probably exceeded only by Kingerlee who participated heavily in the domestic building of North Oxford and in speculative building of house property elsewhere in Oxford, areas of business which Symm eschewed: the census showed Kingerlee employed over 200 people. But it is clear that the number employed varied significantly according to the work in hand and the time of the year. Apart from a small permanent staff, skilled tradesmen and labourers were engaged as required. A heavy programme required large numbers; in September 1884, for instance, as many as 186 men were working at the University Laboratories in what was to become the Science Area, and a further thirty-three elsewhere. They were laid off when the job was completed or work ceased due to weather conditions; in January 1885 the number was down to 132. The men had to fend for themselves, look for other work or wait in idleness. In college work the peak of activity coincided with the summer Long Vacation. Hours of work were also variable and if those were reduced, the men's earnings fell. By the mid 1880s, as a Saturday half-day became general, the normal week had fallen to fifty five hours but overtime was common, even up to sixty-six hours on occasion; in lean periods in winter men might be paid only for thirty-five hours. A skilled mason or joiner got an hourly rate of $7\frac{1}{2}$ d. and could receive £1.10s or more per week: the labourer might get 4d and a wage of between 15s and £1. There were no paid holidays and holidays would be limited to a day at Christmas, Good Friday, Bank Holidays, and a day or two at Fair Time. In December 1879 Mr. Symm gave

Symm's stone yard, Cromwell Street, St. Ebbes, close to Christ Church, a major client

his staff Christmas gifts - a cash bonus which in total amounted to £10.4s.6d., perhaps 2s per person, modest enough but acceptable by Victorian standards.

Symm and Thomas Howard withdrew from the Partnership in 1884. Symm retained his ownership of the yards and other properties and his loan to the firm but his active involvement ceased. The ongoing Partners, Thomas Axtell and Benjamin Hart, had by then built up a capital in the business of £2,250 each.

Symm lived on at 34 St. Giles'; bereaved by the death of his daughter and then his wife, he died in July 1887 near Allendale, his birthplace, aged seventy eight. His body was brought back to Oxford to be buried alongside his wife and daughter in a vault at the Wesleyan Chapel he had built. He left an estate of £19,964, not the largest of Victorian fortunes but substantial for Oxford and the equivalent of about £1,200,000 in today's money. His wealth passed

*The old Bartlemas Chapel, off
Cowley Road in Pether's Farm*

mainly to the descendants of his sister and brother. Part of the estate was the leasehold property at 34 St. Giles'; this was now purchased by the ongoing Partnership, renamed Symm and Company, for £1,200, let to a tenant for £25 per year and insured for £1,000. The Partnership also purchased for £700 the lease of four terrace houses in Little Clarendon Street, these being let to tenants paying in total £18 rent per annum: as with St. Giles', household property at the time gave only a low if reliable yield. Finally, from Symm's assets, the Partnership bought the lease of the joinery workshops and yard at Little Clarendon Street for £800, paying a ground rent of £70 per annum.

These bald facts convey little of the personality and character of Joshua Symm. Pious, prudent, industrious, frugal, these are all words that would describe his lifestyle. As an employer he was strict, demanding, straightforward and paternal in his relationships with his men. He had some prominence in Oxford and was a Charity trustee in the company of such eminent men as Henry Acland, Regius Professor of Medicine, William Spooner, later to become Warden of New College, and George Morrell, the brewer, as well as other Oxford worthies. It would be in the Methodist community and within the building trade that he would be best known and most respected. Above all, he was an outstanding stonemason, with no large ambitions beyond the successful pursuit of his craft and his trade and the way of life associated with it. The fine buildings with which he is most associated, and notably Exeter College Chapel, are his best memorial.

Hertford College: new hall about to be built

An early project for the new partnership, Symm and Company, completed in 1888. The Hall and Gateway joined the two Catte Street blocks built by Evans in 1822 (Oxford Almanack 1892)

A. ERNEST SMITH 1891.

Etched by A. ERNEST SM

THE NEW HALL OF HERTFORD COLLEGE

CHAPTER

A NEW PARTNERSHIP
SYMM and COMPANY: 1887-1926

Following Joshua Symm's death the new Partnership continued to flourish. Its reputation for craft stonework and carpentry and reliable service was firmly established. Thomas Axtell and his colleague, Benjamin Hart, had a relationship of trust and respect, where each played a complementary role. Axtell was now regarded in Oxford as the acknowledged expert on stonework. The college and University building market remained active. New and enlarged buildings were still a feature as the institutions continued to grow and required larger and more modern accommodation. But as age and deterioration took their toll of the old local stone, not least because of new sources of pollution, restoration of the old fabric became an urgent, even fashionable, requirement - a form of activity where Symm in particular quickly established expertise.

Apart from the ongoing routine work for its major clients, a number of other important projects came along. One, in 1890, was the church of St. Matthew in Grandpont, an impressive Victorian gothic building. Here the prime mover was Canon A.M.W. Christopher of St. Aldate's who would be familiar with Symm and Company's expertise: the architect was Canon Christopher's cousin, J.T. Christopher, who had worked with the Partnership on St. Aldate's. St. Matthew's was a huge church to seat six hundred in a growing but poor part of Oxford, built on land given by Brasenose College and largely financed by an appeal launched by Canon Christopher. Funds were short and Symm's estimate, the lowest submitted, was £6,520; a circular from Canon Christopher in June 1890, with the walls some feet from the ground, shows that the total was already almost half subscribed, with £3,267 paid and promised. A further appeal raised the balance and the church was completed. Symm's stone carvers had an opportunity for some lively work on the exterior with its stone heads, gargoyles and floral decoration. The spacious interior featured a fine barrel roof in the chancel, vigorous stone carving in the reredos, and a carved oak dog-tooth frieze to the roof as well as elaborate wood carving in the pulpit and choir stalls, the latter the work of Symm's joiners.

Other work in Oxford included the restoration of the tower and south front of All Saints' Church in 1888, followed some years later in 1906-07 by the refacing of other weathered parts of the building on the other three sides. The stone front of Cornbury Park, near Charlbury, was refaced around 1890.

St. Matthew's Church, Grandpont, near the Thames in flood, 1890s

All Saints' Church restoration, 1888

opposite page:
The Hall at Lincoln College and its timber roof, restored in 1889

St. Barnabas' Church in Jericho was enlarged and repaired, new classrooms added to its school, and a Parish Institute built in 1892. 1891 saw major work at the Radcliffe Infirmary where Symm was responsible for extending some of the wards and a complete improvement of sanitary arrangements throughout the hospital, which remained an important client in the period through 1893. Another Oxford hospital in Cowley St. John was the subject of new buildings between 1889 and 1891. Symm was doing work at Radley College in 1891, building a new wing with five classrooms. In 1893 they began work on the Christ Church Choir School to the designs of H.W. Moore.

The association with T.G. Jackson that had begun at the Bodleian Library in 1876 continued in 1889 at Lincoln College where they restored the Dining Hall and opened up the marvellous timber roof, long hidden by a plaster ceiling, and in 1893-96 at the University Church of St. Mary with the replacement of all the pinnacles on the church and spire (Jackson's book, *St. Mary the Virgin, Oxford*, resulted from the work). More work followed in 1895-96 at All Saints' Church, refloored and reseated to a higher standard to serve as the City Church; and in 1897 at Carfax Tower (left on its own when St. Martin's, the older City Church, was demolished in 1896), repaired with a new stair-turret and parapets.

Also to Jackson's designs, Symm built what came to be known as the Acland Hospital at 25 Banbury Road in 1896. This consisted of large wings to Northgate House, providing private wards and nurses' rooms. 50 years later in 1936 Lord Nuffield paid for the original nucleus, Northgate House of c1840, to be pulled down and replaced by the present brick Georgian style front block.

Previously in 1867 the firm had built the adjoining 23 Banbury Road, now Felstead House, the Acland consulting rooms, for the Revd. S.J. Holmes to E.G. Bruton's design. Between 1898 and 1907 Symm did more building in the University Museum complex when they won the contract for the Morphological Laboratory and subsequently for the Pathological Laboratory. They were to do more work at the Pitt Rivers Museum a few years later, having originally built the museum in 1885-86.

While all this work reflects the firm's specialisation, for the most part on fine building as distinct from house-building or the general market for commercial building, Symm from time to time dipped into the more competitive

areas, building shops in Queen Street for instance, making alterations to the Golden Cross Inn, Cornmarket, remodelling the premises of the Oxfordshire and Berkshire Bank in King Edward Street, or converting the Ship Hotel in Broad Street into lodgings. An unusual project was at Wolvercote Paper Mill in the 1890s where new buildings for additional paper machines, a boiler house and tall chimney were constructed. In 1898 the firm built a very large private house, now the School of Geography, for Dr. Mee on the corner of Mansfield Road and Jowett Walk; the architect, T.G. Jackson's son Basil, had his father's sweeping confidence but lacked his skill at combining motifs of diverse origins. An unusual project at the turn of the century was the extension of the Oxford University Boat Club on the bank of the Isis.

Extension to boathouse, Oxford University Boat Club

Competition remained vigorous, especially in the general commercial market and in work on public buildings. Kingerlee became prominent with major contracts such as the Central Girls Board School in New Inn Hall Street in 1900 and the New Theatre in George Street. Kingerlee also rebuilt the George Street Congregational Chapel at this time, built mews and stables at the Randolph Hotel, and seems to have succeeded Symm as the general builder at the Radcliffe Infirmary. This Oxford firm also made important extensions to the Taylor Institution in 1893, building on the site of the yard of the now defunct firm of Wyatt. The Oxford firms of Wooldridge and Curtis both won major school jobs, the former for the Central Boys School at Gloucester Green in 1900, the latter for the City Technical School. Benfield and Loxley now became an important new name among Oxford builders, one that has survived under varying ownership; they were building at Magdalen College School and at the Choir School in the 1890s, extending County Hall in 1896 and later won important contracts for University Departmental buildings in Parks Road. Wooldridge, now in partnership with Simpson, built St. Michael's church in Summertown where the contract for the first phase was £7,866, and a prestigious scheme at the Dragon School. In 1893-94 the contract for important new City buildings, the Town Hall and Library in St. Aldate's, designed by H.T. Hare, was awarded to Parnell of Rugby. Parnell, a long established outsider on the Oxford scene also won the large contract worth £21,000 financed by the Drapers Company to build the Radcliffe Science Library in South Parks Road in 1900.

opposite page:
Restoration of the tower and spire of the University Church of St. Mary the Virgin, a major project in 1893-96. Erecting and maintaining the timber scaffolding would itself be a major undertaking

Competition did Symm no harm; the Partnership had its niche and secure reputation and its ambitions, modest but prestigious, were met. Indeed the financial results achieved since 1884 would only be regarded as highly satisfactory. The turnover - and this was cash received for work completed - was fairly stable, ranging between £20,000 and £25,000 yearly. While balance sheets and profit and loss statements have not survived, the cash balances held in the Bank and the drawings of the Partners were a good indication of the firm's profitability. In February 1886, before Joshua Symm's death, the Bank balance was £8,335: Axtell and Hart were sufficiently confident to withdraw £1,200 each. By February 1889, although substantial payments had been made to Symm's estate the balance was £7,006 and the Partners drew another £500 each. By 1891, the balance reached £10,537 prompting the purchase of £3,000 nominal Oxford Corporation 3 per cent Stock. Drawings of £2,000 each took place in 1895 and in the period 1897-1900 a further £2,200 each was taken out. The balance in February 1901 was £7,650.

Thomas Axtell died in December 1901 at the age of seventy five, still living as he had for most of his working life in St. Ebbe's. In 1880 he had moved from the house and shop in Commercial Road to No. 17 Speedwell Street, a larger terrace house in the third block west from St. Aldate's. After Joshua Symm, he was the respected gifted craftsman in stone who brought a wealth of experience and knowledge of the finest building practices of the day to the service of his clients; he preserved and extended the Partnership's outstanding reputation in its field. But more than this he had the managerial and commercial abilities to maintain and develop a successful business. Axtell left a modest fortune, about £15,000, but he founded a dynasty and successive generations of Axtells were to enhance the traditions he had established and to carry the business forward to the present day.

Two of his sons, Thomas Junior and Richard had trained as stonemasons at the London house, Butcher and Axtell of Camberwell, specialist stone sculptors, where there was a long-standing family connection; they carried out the carving at the Cathedral Choir School in 1893. It would be a matter of disappointment that the eldest son, Thomas Junior, did not meet his father's high standards. He joined the firm and worked at Christ Church but he took to drink, behaved irresponsibly and got into debt. Reprimanded by Thomas Senior, the son left in a pique but found the resources and support to start on his own as a builder, trading from 9a St. Aldate's. Indeed he was successful in 1894 in

Speedwell Street in St. Ebbes, where Thomas Axtell lived with his large family from 1880 until his death

winning the contract to build a New Corn Exchange and Fire Station in George Street for the City Council to H.W. Moore's designs, a contract worth £10,888. The following year he secured the contract to build the High School for Boys, also in George Street, working with the architect T.G. Jackson. But his initial success was not sustained; he mismanaged his financial affairs to the verge of bankruptcy, ceased to trade and brought embarrassment , financial and otherwise to his father and family. Thomas was excluded from his father's will and seems to have moved away from Oxford.

In 1883 Thomas's youngest son Alfred had been indentured as an apprentice at the age of fourteen for a term of six years to an Oxford plumber, John Peattie of Kingston Road. His father paid a consideration of £25 to Peattie, and also provided board and lodging and tools to his son, who committed himself not 'to contract Matrimony within the said Term nor play at Cards or Dice Tables.' The indenture goes on 'He shall neither buy nor sell. He shall not haunt Taverns or Playhouses.' Alfred was to receive 2s 6d weekly initially although this sum rose progressively to 14s in the final year of his service. Alfred eventually joined Peattie in partnership, trading as Peattie and Axtell, not only in Oxford from premises at 35 and 36 High Street, but also 1 Gloucester Road, South Kensington, London. Subsequently Alfred continued on his own account, based at 17 Woodstock Road, Oxford. He was succeeded by Tom Howse (eventually H.E. Howse and Company Ltd) which became the forerunner of the present Sharp and Howse Limited. Over many years they did much of Symm's plumbing, supplementing the firm's own team, and eventually joined the Symm group.

Meanwhile it was Richard, the second son, living at 17, Pembroke Street, St. Aldate's, and present at his father's death, who 'took his place'. Thomas Axtell's Partner, Benjamin Hart, now retired, being succeeded by his son, Harry J. Hart known to everyone as 'Bandy' Hart. The younger Axtell and Hart were joined in the new Partnership by Richard Evans, brother-in-law of Axtell, who had started as an apprentice in 1864 and for many years had been Head Foreman of the old concern, but who had been working independently more recently with T.G. Jackson; in 1902 he was living at Settle in Yorkshire where he had been Clerk of Works on the construction of Giggleswick School Chapel; as Jackson relates in his memoirs, this was built without an overall contractor by daywork and sub-contracts. £5,000 capital, held in equal shares, was brought into the new firm, some £2,800 being applied to the purchase

Thomas Axtell junior quarrelled with his father and set up his own building concern. A large project in 1895 was the High School for Boys. Subsequently his business failed and he became estranged from the family

Peattie and Axtell's account to R Macau of University College, 1894

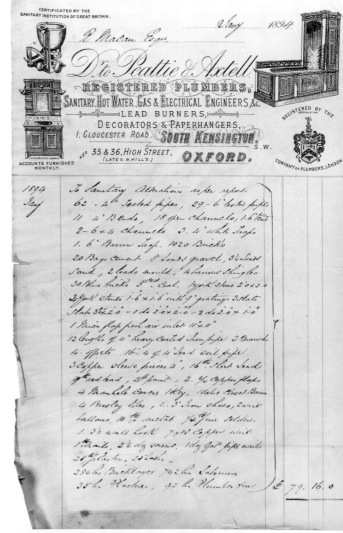

from the old Partnership of the goodwill, stock in trade, and leasehold properties at 34, St. Giles', the yard at 43, Little Clarendon Street, and four cottages along that street. The Partnership agreement of February 1902 reads cautiously: the Partners were to restrict their drawings to £3 weekly out of profits; 25 per cent of each year's profits were to be put in reserve to meet extraordinary losses or capital expenditure on premises, with the desired aim of building a reserve of at least £7,000; the Partners had a defined discretion to hire or dismiss workmen not on the regular staff; they agreed not to become members of any political or social club. The three Partners had different roles: Hart was the administrator who kept the books; Evans probably remained very much in charge of the workforce; Axtell concentrated on preparing estimates and securing business, customer relations and maintaining the very high standards of workmanship particularly in stone that were the firm's hallmark.

The assets of the old Partnership, augmented by the £2,800 received from its successor, were distributed at the time, either to Benjamin Hart or to Thomas Axtell's executors. The total sum distributed was £10,800. Over the life of the old Partnership profits seemed to have averaged about 5 per cent of turnover, the return on capital about 15 per cent. The new Partnership got off to a good start. Accounts survive for three years of trading, as summarised below:

Symm and Co. Trading Accounts

Year ending	Profit £	Drawings £	Bonus £	Balance £
28 February 1903	1,136	450	300	5,906
28 February 1904	1,526	624	300	6,508
28 February 1905	2,016	624	300	7,600

The Partners had raised their drawings to £4 weekly with an individual bonus of £100, not exactly riches but enough to keep one or two servants and a comfortable household. And they enjoyed their status and independence and freedom to pursue their business interest.

The early years of the new Partnership are especially associated with major restoration to some of Oxford's most precious ancient buildings. In 1906 T.G. Jackson as architect and Symm as builder, restored the stone balustrade of the Old Ashmolean. The same team were then given the task of modifying the adjacent Sheldonian Theatre, to lessen the risk and danger of fire, rebuilding the stairs to one of the rostra. Three years later, again working to the direction of Jackson, Symm carried out major restoration, replacing the balustrade, pedestals and vase ornaments. The work continuing until 1911. Meanwhile between 1907 and 1909 the west and then the south front and

Sheldonian Cupola under repair, c1910

finally the east front of the Clarendon Building were partly refaced with Clipsham stone. This work under the architect J.R. Wilkins, was on an agreed scale: the charge for fixing the dressed Clipsham stone, including cutting out the defective stonework, varied from 10s 6d per cubic foot for the main cornice and pediment, 9s for jambs and arches of windows down to 7s for plain ashlar. Day by day the work was meticulously recorded for monthly settlement by the Curators and their architect, J.R. Wilkins. Scaffolding was quite an item, £30 up to 20 feet, and another £30 'up to the top'.

The largest restoration task of the period was at Christ Church where, beginning in 1908, extensive repairs were made to the St. Aldate's front including Tom Tower; Clipsham and Doulting stone were again the material. This work extended over several years with building activity a familiar site along St. Aldate's. For several months Tom Tower was clothed in an intricate and cleverly build framework of timber scaffolding which itself cost £300, and can be admired in Muirhead Bone's

Muirhead Bone's drawing of Tom Tower, Christ Church, clothed in intricate scaffolding during the major restoration that started in 1908 (Oxford Almanack 1910)

drawing used as the headpiece for the University Almanack in 1910. Such a framework, creaking and groaning in the wind, had to be checked and wedges and ropes tightened regularly. (Incidentally, when timber scaffolding was eventually replaced by steel later this century many operatives, who had been used to the protection and security of large pole enclosures, were reluctant to climb the new thin light framework, which, appearing more open to the skies, seemed quite perilous!) Most of the work on the St. Aldate's facade was measured work costed on the basis of the cubic footage and type of stone replaced, but some, for a variety of repair tasks such as replacing gutters and rainwater pipes, fixing chimney pots, forming new cesspools, painting sashes and frames,was daywork charged on the basis of time worked and materials used. Meticulous accounts were submitted relating to the volume and type of stonework replaced, or the daywork tasks performed. The total cost of measured work for the St. Aldate's facade and Tom Tower amounted to just over £14,600; daywork was several £100's extra. This work resulted in the architect W.D. Carõe writing *Wren and Tom Tower* (1923).

At the same time Symm, working with Alfred Axtell, now in business on his own account, were putting bathrooms and showers into the basements of Tom and Peckwater Quads and into Meadow Buildings, a considerable undertaking. Here cost was a consideration and to save on the estimate of

approaching £2,000 the College scaled down its requirement from eighteen baths and five showers to eleven baths and four showers between the three buildings: no doubt an advance on previous facilities but somewhat inadequate by today's standards. Interestingly, Axtell did all the plumbing and supplied the baths, Symm adding 15 per cent to his costs in their final bill.

Symm had been repairing and refacing parts of the old buildings of University College in the 1880s, adding new accommodation and improvements. Now in 1903 they were given the delicate task of extending the 17th century Hall and opening up the original roof which was then reconstructed with many new timbers to the original design of 1656. A bridge across Logic Lane, the subject of intense controversy between the College and the City of Oxford, was built in 1905, and then the Front Quad and the High Street frontage were extensively restored between 1907 and 1910.

Another sensitive restoration project at this time (1905) was at St. John's College where five of the columns in the Canterbury Quad were replaced in Portland stone. Similar work was carried out at Wadham during the 1900s: restoration of pinnacles to the Hall and Library; replacement of the roof of the Warden's House; repairs to the Chapel and Hall. In 1910 Symm was restoring the tower at Corpus Christi College; in 1909 and 1910 dismantling and reconstructing the cupola at Queen's College in Portland stone, and renovating the clock tower in Clipsham stone. For many years Symm was asked to send a team of workmen to help stir the vats when Queen's was brewing its college ale, a common occurrence at the time. That apart, these

Symm masons at the top of Tom Tower

opposite page:
The St. Aldate's front, Christ Church in 1909. At the time it was estimated some twenty seven miles of scaffolding poles were used in the structure

St. John's College, Canterbury Quad: restoration to stone columns (Oxford Almanack 1937)

Architect H.W. Moore's letter to the Master of University College regarding Symm's estimate for the extension of the Hall, 1903

Rebuilding the cupola at Queen's College was a sensitive project in 1910

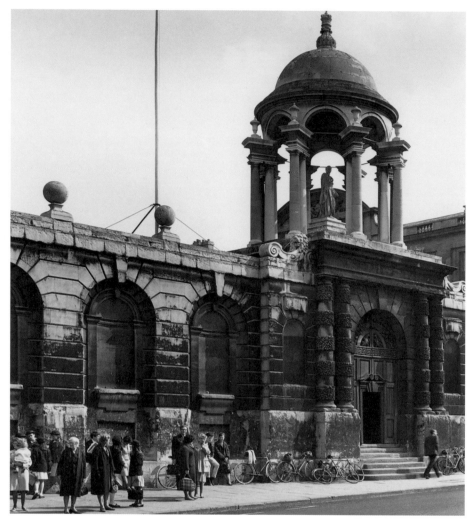

were the kind of tasks which, of all the Oxford builders, Symm was best qualified to execute sensitively. In all these restorations, certain common principles were followed, best summarised by Richard Evans; he wrote: 'We have endeavoured faithfully and carefully to reproduce the correct details of the old work; to select the best quality of stone and to see that the stone was laid or fixed on its natural bed, that is not face or joint bedded; also not to take away more than necessary any of the old stone work.'

Merton College returned as a client in this busy period with a major project in 1906 to construct the new St. Alban Hall block, designed by Basil Champneys, with fourteen sets of rooms and seven bathrooms. The former Warden's Lodgings was converted into a handsome new Senior Common Room and Bursary. Everything here was done to the highest standard, the stone carefully chosen, oak panelling, oak flooring, a Greek marble fireplace in the new Junior Common Room. In 1911 Symm restored the Chapel and east and south garden fronts of the Fellows' Quadrangle, and strengthened and reslated the roof of the Library. (Major restoration work on the Chapel and Library has continued to the present day.)

Worcester College turned to Symm following an extensive and serious fall of the stone external cornice above the Chapel. The parapet was then rebuilt including the cornice and pediment of the Library. The following year Symm did significant work on the Provost's Lodgings and redecorated the Hall and Library. (Symm later carried out major improvements at the Lodgings in 1962 for the incoming Provost, Lord Franks.)

The character of this exceptionally busy period is revealed by site notebooks which have survived. Apart from the major projects, Symm was in constant demand for smaller repairs, modifications and improvements to the fabric and facilities of those colleges with whom the closest relationship had developed, Christ Church, Wadham, University, Exeter, Merton to name the most loyal. Richard Axtell or Richard Evans were always on call from the Bursars and other senior Members of these institutions, to give advice, consultation or estimates.

Symm's specialised skills had their securest outlet in the colleges. There is some indication that in major projects the firm had become expensive and perhaps uncompetitive. Thus in a competitive tender for a new church at New Headington to the designs of Sir Arthur Blomfield in 1908, Symm quoted £3,895 to be undercut by many others including Estcourt, Kingerlee, Benfield and Loxley (£3,549) and Franklin of Deddington (£3,389). Another major competition for the Electrical Engineering Laboratory in 1909, to T.G. Jackson's designs, saw Symm quote £12,968 with Parnell of Rugby coming in lowest among 12 tenders at £10,797. For additions to Lady Margaret Hall, Symm quoted £8,042 and lost the work to Benfield and Loxley whose tender was £7,154. On a smaller job for the Wadham College Cricket Pavilion Symm quoted £746 against Benfield and Loxley £513. The Partners were probably

Horse and cart, or hand cart, were the builder's transport at the turn of the century

not too concerned, although if work was short they would cut their estimate to make sure of getting the job; this seems to have been the case with the Morphological Laboratory where an estimate of £7,737 was reduced to £7,077 when tendered.

By February 1908 the Partnership's retained capital had grown to £11,104 of which about £2,800 seems to have been cash, about the same stock, and the balance accounts receivable and work in progress. Colleges predominated as clients but there was a steady flow of work outside the University, decoration of large private homes in North Oxford, Iffley and Headington, shops and offices in the centre. In February

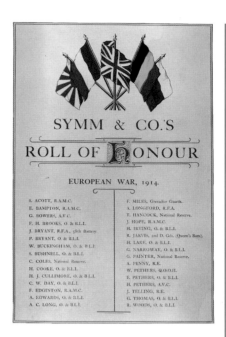

1908 Symm and Co. had a workforce, regular and casual, of 118 including thirty masons, fifteen carpenters, four bricklayers, two plasterers, six painters, fifty five labourers, two carters and four clerks. The weekly payroll was £175. Hours of work were now much reduced from Joshua Symm's day, 8½ weekdays and 5 on Saturday, a total of forty seven and a half hours. On daywork time was charged at rates between 10d an hour for a painter or a slater, 7d for a labourer and 6d for a boy, while the men were paid at rates about one-third lower, the mark-up being 50 per cent. The workforce varied with the college calendar with much of the repair/improvement activity crowded into the vacations. Accidents were recorded, fortunately few; one labourer was hit on the head by a falling bucket; another fell from scaffolding to die 3 hours later. Other incidents were typical: the steward at Exeter suspected one of Symm's men working at the College had stolen a bottle of cherry brandy; the men were assembled and told that if anyone were found out having taken the brandy they would never be employed again; the steward was apparently satisfied that Symm's workmen were not responsible!

By the time of the Great War the Partnership capital had probably reached £20,000. The character of the business is revealed by the bare statistics of the accounts for 1913/1914: receipts from completed work were £17,412 against direct expenses £8,412 wages and £5,355 materials; after carriage and carting the contribution to overhead and profit was £3,069. Overheads included many items such as rent, insurance, office expenses but totalled only £1,167. This was a lean, tight operation and achieved a profit of £1,902, nearly 11% of sales; the profit, of course, had to meet the remuneration of the three Partners. Assets at the end of February 1914 included £9,394 work in progress or receivables. The client list is interesting and representative: work in progress, partly covered by payments on account included the Curators of the Bodleian Library for restoration work on the Radcliffe Camera and construction of the subway connecting the Library with the Camera; Corpus Christi College where Symm was restoring the Library; Merton College Chapel for work on the pinnacles. Receivables were due from Christ Church (£1,215), Merton, Queen's and the Bishop of Oxford who owed £349. These, of course were all reliable debtors, if occasionally slow payers. Many of the receivables were small sums owed by the Dean, Sub-Dean, Steward, Treasurer, Archdeacon or various Canons of Christ Church who seem to have had separate accounts. This was very much a traditional business, with a close indeed intimate relationship of trust and confidence with its main clients.

The onset of the Great War brought all work but routine college maintenance to an abrupt halt. By 1916 the accounts show greatly reduced activity and indeed one may suppose many of Symm's workforce were on active service.

opposite page:
Symm had carried out major restoration of the Bodleian Library between 1876-84. Further work, of the most delicate character, to replace damaged woodwork, was carried out in 1923

One incident records the old connection maintained; in 1918 the bell-clapper in Tom Tower at Christ Church broke and Great Tom would have been silent but for two of Symm 's workmen, who were asked to ring the bell by hand, 101 times nightly at 9.05 p.m. 101 was the original number of students when the College was founded by Henry VIII; the tolling of the bell was a warning for them to leave the alehouses of the town and return to the College before the gates closed for the night. The workmen, father and son, were told to make the chimes sound like the normal evening toll; they practised with a drumstick, unheard, to get the timing right; on the first night 'the dons went mad' because the bell was rung 103 times by mistake; thereafter they were given 101 marbles and two candle boxes so that they got the number right. After two weeks this campanology ceased when the new bell-clapper came from London.

In 1922 Symm carried out a major survey of decayed stonework at Merton College, drawing on their long experience to recommend treatment. A subsequent testimonial from Bursar Thring refers to Merton College employing Symm and Co. 'as builders for a great many years and they also do the whole of the work at Christ Church, including the Cathedral, and many other colleges. They are thoroughly trustworthy people with plenty of common sense to carry out any new idea.' Woodwork, as well as stonework, remained the firm's speciality. In 1923 they returned to the Bodleian laying a new oak floor in the Binder's room and repairing/replacing fine woodwork, throughout the building. Renovation and redecoration of the Radcliffe Camera followed, for which Axtell was personally thanked by the Curators, delighted at 'the admirable way' in which 'a complicated and exacting task' had been completed in time for the first day of term. Symm were working at the Bodleian during the General Strike in 1926 when inspection of the roof timbers of Duke Humphrey's Library revealed serious decay due to death watch beetle; the subsequent delicately handled restoration attracted recognition in the national press, always in an authentic manner, faithful as far as possible to the original.

This phase in Symm's history, the second Partnership as it may be termed, which had maintained the reputation and traditions of the Firm now established over 100 years, ended with the retirement of Richard Evans in 1926. Probably to lessen the risk of the Partners, a limited company was then formed with a share capital of £15,000. Harry Hart became Chairman although Richard Axtell was the moving spirit: they were joined by their sons Leonard Hart and Dudley Axtell as Directors with Richard's younger son, Graham Axtell joining the Board a few years later in 1933. The modern phase of Symm and Co., the Limited company, begins at this time.

The Radcliffe Camera

Charlbury Road, Oxford, 1922

opposite page:
All Souls College: restoration of
Hawksmoor's twin towers, 1923-24

CHAPTER

TO THE PRESENT DAY
SYMM and COMPANY: 1926 - 1998

The new limited company started its life at a difficult time. Along with most other forms of business, building activity was affected by the deep depression in industry and trade in the late 1920s and subsequent years. Many building concerns failed in this period.

The Oxford colleges were short of funds and major projects of extension or restoration were forgotten or postponed*. Essential maintenance and repair continued with the major college clientele and at institutions like the Bodleian. Symm and Company retrenched, reducing staff and overhead expenses. In the financial year 1930-31, after the Directors had taken salaries of £1,500, the dividend was passed and a balance of £551 carried forward in the accounts. In the following year the Directors took a salary reduction to £800, and the dividend was again passed, with the balance carried forward being reduced to £55. Harry Hart retired as Chairman in the following year, 1932-33, when the company made a loss, Richard Axtell now becoming Chairman. This was the lowest ebb, with queues of unemployed building workers waiting

St. Edmund Hall: Principal Emden, the architect, R. Feilding Dodd and Dudley R. Axtell (extreme right) watch Archbishop Lang bless the new Canterbury Building, 1934.

at the gates of the Home Yard each morning in the forlorn hope of finding a job. To carry itself forward the company was able to negotiate an overdraft facility with its bankers, the first time in its history that its own capital had not been sufficient to finance its assets. The firm became busier in the mid 1930s. A significant if small project was the Canterbury Building for St. Edmund Hall in 1934-35.

However difficult the times, Symm could always find a place for young men with appropriate skills and motivation. Some of the men who joined the company at this period, and remained with it until their retirement, had come to Oxford from the depressed areas in desperation, bringing craft skills learned in the shipyards and collieries and tramping in search of work, sleeping in doss-houses or the hedgerows. Jack Norton, for example, apprenticed in Barrow-in-Furness, having left home in search of work found it with Symm in Oxford at this time; he went on to become a supervisor and remained with the firm until retirement. Oxford, Slough, West London generally, stimulated by the expanding car industry and by new light industry, became attractive to migrant skilled men and general labourers; once they were in work, their families followed. As

*There was no Government financial support until after the Second World War.

Erecting scaffolding at the Bodleian Library, 1946

activity picked up by the late 1930s, Symm's working week had fallen to forty six hours and skilled tradesmen were being paid £3 to £4 weekly and labourers £2.

The outbreak of war in 1939 inevitably reduced activity. Richard Axtell's sons both joined the services as did many of the workforce. Little of note occurred. After the war, when Richard Axtell died in 1948, the next generation assumed control through Richard's sons, Dudley and Graham and Harry Hart's son, Leonard. Dudley Axtell (1903-1961) had joined the firm in 1926. Graham Axtell (1910-1988), seven years younger than his brother, had been trained with local architect, H.S. Rogers and surveyors, Henry Cooper & Son, before joining Symm in 1933; this background and his wartime experience in the Royal Engineers brought into the firm professional and management skills not always to be found within building companies. The leadership of Symm was now well prepared for an exceptionally busy period. A fire in 1950 which substantially destroyed the Home Yard - by then mainly given over to joinery

Home Yard, destroyed by fire in 1950

and offices - was only a temporary setback. In 1951, to broaden the range of services under direct control, the firm strengthened its association with the plumbing and heating business reformed at the beginning of the century by Thomas Axtell's third son, Alfred, a business now trading as H.E. Howse. Symm acquired a half share in the newly incorporated company and was later to take the whole of the equity.

The Axtell brothers were fully engaged, meeting and liaising with clients, both regular and new, preparing schemes and drawings, taking off measured quantities and preparing estimates and submitting tenders. Once a project was accepted they would manage it to completion, although delegating day to day supervision to a subordinate manager or foreman. They would monitor the accounts submitted for stage and final payments. All these, of course, were the tasks of managing an active building firm. Dudley Axtell died in 1961, Graham then becoming Chairman and Managing Director: he introduced both his own sons, Malcolm and Peter, into the business shortly afterwards.

Family continuity in management was matched among those employed by the firm. By the 1950s Symm had increased its work force to its traditional size, that is upwards of 150 men, mainly carpenters, joiners, stonemasons and painters with Howse employing its own plumbers and building services specialists additionally. By 1966 there were 166 men on the payroll, living in St. Ebbe's or Jericho close to the centre of Oxford but a few coming from as far away as Woodstock or Abingdon; most still walked or cycled to work. Many of the work force belonged to families that had been associated with Symm for two or even three generations; family continuity in craft work where materials, methods and tools had seen little change, gave a sense of on-going stability and great pride in upholding the traditions and reputation of the firm.

The post-war period was to provide many opportunities. The great challenge for the University as a whole was the restoration of the heritage of fine building, much in shabby, deplorable and even dangerous condition, the

Propped timber-framed facade of Wymans in Abingdon, 1952

Alington Room, University College.
French walnut panelling with cedar
of Lebanon ceiling. Architect
Sir Albert Richardson RA

result of age, decay, erosion and pollution. Not merely restoration of the old fabric became an urgent necessity, but continued modernisation of older facilities - central heating, electric installations, improved toilet and sanitary arrangements, modernised kitchens and the like - and the substantial enlargement of rooms, libraries, laboratories and teaching facilities to cope with a greatly increased undergraduate population.

The work of the Oxford Historic Buildings Fund between 1957 and 1974 is fully described in W.J. Oakeshott's record, *Oxford Stone Restored* (1975). Symm, with other restoration specialists, played a major part; indeed the resources of all these firms and their skilled craftsmen were fully extended for many years. Highly respected in the City and the building trade, Graham Axtell's expert knowledge of historic stonework including care and restoration was in particular demand. Some of the colleges, Magdalen being an example, employed their own teams of skilled men who were continuously engaged over many years. Others used the firms who had worked on their buildings

94

Old Warden's Hall Merton College:
full restoration of previously hidden
medieval timber roof

Carving boss, Percy Quick

Merton College Chapel: full
restoration of the east window

for a century or more. Thus Symm and Company was heavily involved at Christ Church and Merton, where the more well endowed colleges did not need to call on the University's Fund, and at University, Oriel, Pembroke and Worcester.

At Christ Church, Symm, with other specialist concerns, again restored further phases of the St. Aldate's front and the base of Tom Tower between 1963 and 1966 going on to restore the facades of the Great Quadrangle, Great Hall, Cathedral and Chapter House, and the rear elevations of Peckwater and Canterbury Quadrangles. Such a massive programme, much of it involving refurbishment, internal alterations and improvements, as well as replacement or cleaning of the old stonework, was to run through into the 1980s; it culminated in the restoration of the bell tower, Wolsey Tower, a century after it had been built by Joshua Symm. Not surprisingly the Company had an

North elevation of Cathedral, Christ Church, following stone restoration, 1980s

opposite page:
Tom Tower, Christ Church, following stone restoration, 1960s

The Becket Window (c1320) Cathedral, Christ Church, after complete renewal of stonework, 1981

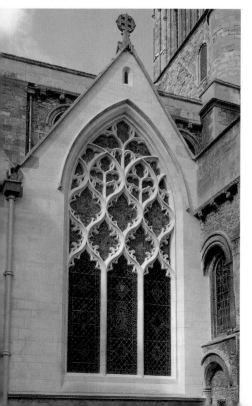

Wolsey Tower, Christ Church, following major stone restoration and renewal, 1977-80. Above, is a corner turret from the tower and below a scroll from a 'time capsule', embedded in the structure

almost permanent team of workmen based at Christ Church throughout this period. Their stonemasonry foreman, Tony Walker MBE., became a familiar figure around the establishment, well known and respected by senior College personalities; he would explain his work in illustrated talks to the University *alumni*. Following tradition, the heads of colleges, Symm and other associated personalities are immortalised in the new stone bosses carved to replace those where original detail had been eroded beyond accurate replication.

APS Masonry personalities, immortalised high up on Magdalen Tower

Graham J. Axtell beside his carved boss, St. Aldate's front, Christ Church.

left: Wolsey Tower gargoyles awaiting fixing

University College: stone parapet restoration, 1960

Another major programme was carried out at University College where, after cleaning by fine-spray water washing, much of the ashlar, plinths, mouldings and chimney stacks needed replacement in Clipsham or other stone. Symm carried out much of the restoration; their original estimate for the work at the College, £104,000, proved remarkably accurate when the programme was completed.

Restoration at Worcester, to which the Historic Buildings Fund contributed £130,000, was a further major Symm assignment at this period. Oakeshott's

University College: before and after restoration,' 1960s

description suggests almost a virtual rebuilding of much of the college. The work here coincided with major alterations and internal and external refurbishment to the impressive 18th century Provost's Lodgings in readiness for their occupation by Sir Oliver Franks (later Lord Franks), the incoming Provost. The firm was familiar with work on the residences of college heads; it had built new Rector's Lodgings at Exeter in the 1850s, the first of many similar tasks. In the 1950s it secured a contract to build new Provost's Lodgings for Queen's College. The architect here, Raymond Erith, had

The Library, Worcester College, following complete stone restoration, 1960s. The use of blue veined Clipsham stone was a feature

The Provost's Lodgings, Queen's College, 1959

designed the building in Georgian style with much of the construction having to be undertaken according to Georgian period techniques; the local press described the finished building as appearing 'faultless'. Symm went on to build the Principal's residence at St. Hilda's, designed by Sir Albert Richardson RA. to a simple but elegant Regency style, and then in 1962-63 new Warden's

Lodgings for Merton College, to a contemporary design by the London architects, Carden and Godfrey. For the men engaged, the work at Merton was memorable for its coincidence with an exceptionally severe winter when for three months outside work was virtually at a standstill. Symm was fortunate to be contracted to clear up deep snow from Oxford streets and cart it to Port Meadow: when the thaw came they were inevitably busy with burst pipes and the like.

At Oriel College, a relatively new college client, Symm also maintained a

above:
Principal's Lodgings, St. Hilda's College, 1954.
above left:
New Warden's Lodgings: Merton College, 1963

opposite page:
The 1960s restoration at Worcester College continued with the Terrace Building and Provost's Lodgings

team of men on the premises throughout the 1950s and 60s, under the charge of a foreman carpenter. They were able to cope with all the college's on-going building needs, from modest tasks like replacing a bookshelf to major alterations. Their work was augmented during the restoration programme; Symm could provide all the necessary expertise and architects or surveyors were rarely involved. A major task here was the reinstatement of the Wyatt Building, housing the Senior Library, which had been gutted by a devastating fire on 7 March 1949. A new copper sheet roof was provided over steel

Ornamental lead rainwater head

Devastating fire damage, Oriel College Library, 1949

The restored Library, Oriel College

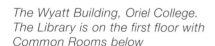

The Wyatt Building, Oriel College. The Library is on the first floor with Common Rooms below

rafters. More recently Symm's fine decoration section carried out the specialist refurbishment and redecoration of the two 18th century Senior Common Rooms beneath the Library, working closely with the celebrated interior designer, John Fowler of the famous London-based interior designers, Colefax and Fowler. Symm was involved in further traditional decorating projects with John Fowler including at Christ Church Library and Deanery, Ditchley Park and Adwell House throughout the 1960/70s.

Active and increasingly prominent in this period, and working closely with Symm, was the specialist stone masonry business, Axtell and Perry. This partnership was founded in 1922 by William Axtell, a stonemason and distant relation of the Symm Axtells, whose early career had begun at Symm, and Harold Perry. Axtell and Perry was to carry out much of the post-war college stone restoration. Eventual collaboration with Symm some years later involved the temporary secondment of skilled craftsmen and the supply of worked stone. Successful working relationships between the heads of the two businesses led to a formal merger in 1972, with the new Axtell Perry Symm Masonry Ltd. (APS Masonry) becoming a subsidiary of the main Symm company.

One of the early major stone restoration projects undertaken by the newly formed APS Masonry was one of Oxford's largest contracts, the significant restoration of the 15th century Great Tower, Magdalen College. Such was its

The Library, Merton College:. Major alteration and oak furniture and fittings, 1958

The Chapel, Trinity College: stone restoration, 1960s (Axtell and Perry Limited) and below: restoration in progress

above left:
Holywell music Room, Oxford:
refurbishment, with
Robert Potter OBE, FRIBA, FSA,
1970s

above right:
Adwell House: Late Georgian
entrance hall and staircase
redecoration with John Fowler

centre:
Window converted to doorway in Tom
Quad, Christ Church

below left:
The Grange, Ramsden: typical
Oxfordshire Cotswold village house
refurbished

below right:
Ferry Pool and Leisure Centre, North
Oxford: under construction, 1975

opposite page:
The Great Tower, Magdalen College:
the stonework to the pinnacles,
pierced balustrade and frieze beneath
was totally renewed, 1980

Stonework to new bridge over River Cherwell, 1930s (Axtell and Perry Ltd)

Carving at Blenheim Palace, Percy Quick

Blenheim Palace, where APS Masonry (and formerly Axtell and Perry Limited) have been involved in stone restoration since the 1930s

height and magnitude that a passenger lift was rigged to convey masons and others involved to and from the upper scaffolding levels. A combination of Clipsham and French limestones was used for both variety and also wearing qualities on such an exposed structure. With the restoration programme spread over several extended phases a generation of Oxford undergraduates was denied sight of this magnificent tower as it was enshrouded in scaffolding for over three years.

While retaining its long and close association with the University and its colleges, Symm maintained clientele elsewhere in the city of Oxford and, especially from the 1970s onwards looked for opportunities for its expertise in a wider market, both elsewhere in the United Kingdom and internationally. Thus they had a long association with the old London and County Bank which became part of the Westminster and subsequently National Westminster Bank. The company had been employed on building or modernising many of the Bank's different premises in Oxford. But, marking this important change in the firm's strategy, in 1970

Symm was called upon to refurbish the neglected and run-down mansion and other buildings in the 4,000 acre Heythrop Park estate which the Bank had acquired for use as a training centre. This was a major project involving stone restoration, reslating and releading roofs, rewiring, complete heating and plumbing renewals, fine internal joinery, painting and decorating, all to a listed historic building.

Heythrop Park, showing later additions, 1970s

Heythrop Park: entrance portico

The work at Heythrop Park, a £750,000 contract, demonstrated Symm's capability to upgrade and refurbish historic buildings to a high standard, in this case within a demanding period of twelve months. This was to prove an important and growing area of business. England, needless to say, had a rich legacy of country houses and gentlemen's seats, not merely in the Home Counties but in the Shires. Many were run down and neglected, the victims of inflation, taxation, and costs of maintenance beyond the resources of their owners. They were often acquired cheaply as residences, schools, hotels, institutions of various kinds. But they needed restoration and refurbishment, to standards depending on the circumstances and needs of the new owners. This was a task for which Symm, with its skills, experience and tradition, was

*Osney Mead stoneworks,
APS Masonry*

admirably suited. Heythrop Park was to be followed by many similar assignments.

Perhaps one of the most high profile historic building projects undertaken since the formation of APS Masonry has been the major stone restoration of the Riverside Terrace elevation of the Palace of Westminster (1985-86) and its now pristine waterfront facade has become an even more familiar sight world-wide. Over fifteen months APS masons spent some 50,000 man hours cutting out decayed stone and working and carving 2,961 new stones for the 940 feet long terrace. To preserve the peace and privacy of Members of

*Thame Park: internal refurbishment,
and re-roofing, 1985*

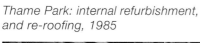

Parliament they worked on site mainly at week-ends only and despite the difficulties of this interrupted programme work was completed ahead of time. Some 200 tonnes of Clipsham stone and the French stone Anstrude Jaune Claire were used, these being delivered, in 20-tonne lorry loads, to the new Osney Mead stoneworks, which, by the late 1960s, had replaced the former Cromwell Street stone yard.

Taplow Court in Buckinghamshire was another country mansion where Symm carried out a successful contract of upgrading, alteration and refurbishment at very short notice. The client here was a Japanese Buddhist organisation (SGI-UK Ltd.); though not the cheapest, Symm was selected following an interview and presentation to both client and architect during which the company's experience on listed historic buildings was probed in depth. The work at Taplow Court, started in 1988, had to be completed in readiness for the official visit of the organisation's world leader eighteen months later; the project was completed on time and the client, clearly pleased with what had been accomplished, congratulated Symm on both the quality of workmanship and the strong team spirit evident amongst the work-force, which had done much to generate confidence that the desired result would be achieved. Further work at Taplow Court continued, by then the European Headquarters, with the total value exceeding £6 million by 1992.

Over its long history, so much of Symm's work has been to tight deadlines.

Palace of Westminster: stone restoration of River Terrace elevation, 1986 (APS Masonry)

*Taplow Court: completion of
temporary roof for major fabric
renewal at roof level, 1990*

The 'Symm Conservatory', and above: view of Le Manoir from the herb garden, Le Manoir aux Quat' Saisons, 1984

Within the University the Long Vacation - a fourteen week period from late June to early October - has been the period when major college projects had to be undertaken; as a general rule all had to be finished and cleaned up before undergraduates returned, with no question of time extension. There were occasions when Symm's workmen were making a prompt start on site as the 'survivors' from the previous night's Commemoration Ball were leaving the college.

A similar tight deadline was set by the world renowned chef, M. Raymond Blanc, when he acquired Great Milton Manor to rehouse his acclaimed North Oxford restaurant in 1983. The intended French-style country house setting, incorporating hotel bedrooms, Le Manoir aux Quat' Saisons, had been awarded two Michelin stars ahead of its opening: the Guide had stated categorically that Le Manoir would be opening on 15th March 1984. Symm was awarded the £450,000 contract late in 1983. Two teams had to cover a twenty-four hour day to ensure a successful outcome, and after many sleepless nights for management and craftsmen together, the complex was in business on the due date. Raymond Blanc returned with two further significant extensions and in recognition of the special relationship built up, the major dining room conservatory, developed and made in Symm workshops, has been named the 'Symm Conservatory'. The £5m further phase III improvement scheme was undertaken in 1997-98.

above:
Merton College, Library: advanced decay on 17th c. stone dormers prior to restoration
right:
Stone dormers fully restored, 1990s

Restoration to Merton College properties in Holywell Street. Before and after

Creation of the Pizza Express restaurant within the historic 'Golden Cross' buildings, 1987

THE FUTURE FOR SYMM

The 1980s and 1990s brought periods of severe recession to the building industry which naturally put pressures on the Symm Group, its management and staff. To a certain extent, these were alleviated through the diversity of services provided by Symm and Company, APS Masonry and Sharp and Howse, so that activity in one area tended to offset slack periods in others. The Group's reputation and close relationships with Oxford colleges, institutions such as the NatWest Bank and other long-standing clients also ensured a flow of restoration and refurbishment work in these difficult times.

The fact that Symm survived and developed during a period which saw the demise of many building companies has repercussions beyond the company itself. For over 180 years, Symm has fostered the craft skills of building through a dedication to the apprenticeship tradition and through ensuring that the quality of workmanship was not compromised. Companies like Symm preserve a range of traditional skills that can all too easily be put at risk by adverse economic pressures or changes in architectural taste. Fortunately, greater attention today to the quality of work and the materials that create the built environment mean that these skills are once again increasingly in demand.

The strength of the Symm Group lies both in the wide diversity of in-house skills it can provide and in the way these skills are managed and utilised. Technology, such as the latest stone cutting and profiling equipment, Computer Aided Design and new machinery for joinery, are used in conjunction with hand skills. This means that the latter are employed where they are most needed, for special features and detailed work requiring particular historical attention and individual artistry. Speed and efficiency, so necessary for today's building and restoration projects, can therefore be applied without losing the ability to enhance and embellish. Symm has been able to market these skills in a way that has increased the range of services

Natural stonework to new premises in Golden Square, London, 1996 (APS Masonry)

Fluting columns, to entasis

Carving Ionic column capital

New oak panelled Library, private residence in Virginia, USA. Detail taken from traditional historic Oxford woodwork, 1983

to clients without over stretching resources. Among the most recent service additions have been 'Interiors' and 'Conservation', making use of the extensive available skills in specialist building and decorative work for internal projects, while in the area of conservation combining building craftsmanship with historical knowledge in the cause of preservation.

Indicators to the future for Symm can be seen in the way that the Group's unique craft skills can be exported, particularly in the area of fine woodwork. Technical expertise and artistry allied to a commitment to achieving period

116

Completing pew end

left:
New Chapel interior, private residence in Virginia, USA, modelled on Shobdon Church in Herefordshire, 1984

Carved oak rails and pulpit awaiting shipment to USA for installation at Grace Episcopal Church, New Bedford, MA, USA, 1992

accuracy have created a demand for Symm workmanship overseas, beginning in the USA. Using the finest hardwoods, Symm is able to produce, ship and install replica historic rooms, such as oak panelled libraries, or single items such as individual purpose-built cabinets. Entire interiors can be exactly replicated if desired, one of the most unusual being the replica of the 18th century 'Strawberry Hill Gothick' church interior at Shobdon, Herefordshire, which was created by Symm for a private client in Virginia.

The wide range of Symm's building disciplines is supported by structured

Lead roof coverings to new Library, Wadham College, 1975 (Sharp and Howse Ltd.)

approaches to project management, which are designed to progress projects rapidly while causing minimum disruption to the client's commercial or private life. A company that is capable of providing anything from major stonework replacement to a specialist skill like limewashing will find a demand for its work, but being known for addressing clients' interests will give it an additional advantage over competitors who do not have a similar reputation.

Symm are good at keeping a discrete and courteous presence whilst working on a project. They have had generations of practice at being accommodating to the academic needs of Oxford colleges. They are also used to dealing with the demands of private property owners great and small for as quiet a life as possible while building work is being carried out.

Calling out the builder could, in many cases, be described by the marketing term 'distress purchase'. In other words, when urgent repairs are required after fire damage or suddenly discovered structural decay, the client is going to need a high level of support and understanding. This is one of the areas covered by a company policy known as 'The Symm Approach', which will be described later.

There is definitely a place in the future, as far as Symm is concerned, for providing a wide range of building disciplines under one banner. The company rarely needs to subcontract core activities, especially when dealing with projects more local to the Oxford area, and therefore can ensure a high level of control over the workforce employed. The Symm Group is prepared to deal with new building and restoration projects of every scale. Thanks to the affiliations with APS Masonry and Sharp and Howse, it can provide specialist building skills for internal and external projects, a full range of crafts, joinery, decoration, stonemasonry, leadwork and building services. All these skills

Building services, Sharp and Howse Limited

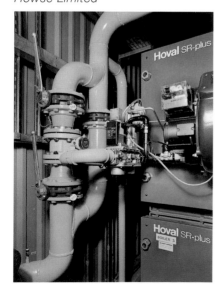

Rover Cowley, Vehicle Preparation Centre: building services installed in record time by Sharp and Howse Limited, 1997

can be brought together under project management and design and build programmes, making for effective lines of communication and efficient project handling. Full project management is a way forward for many schemes, although Symm fully acknowledges that others should remain architect-led.

The Symm Group has in recent years extended its scope far beyond the city of Oxford and includes work on major public and historic buildings such as Blenheim Palace, the Palace of Westminster, Chequers and Uppark, the National Trust property extensively restored after major fire damage. Examples of Symm fine woodwork have crossed the Atlantic to grace residences from New York to Texas. Symm workmanship has been used by Harrods, by hotels and restaurants and by private clients with country estates or living in flats and houses in London, Oxford and other towns and cities. While Symm has

119

Uppark: renewal and painting of windows following fire destruction, 1991

opposite page:
Sheldonian Theatre: Symm returns for further restoration, 1995

often been associated with college restoration or major heritage projects, it should not be forgotten that a large proportion of its work is also on a relatively small scale for private individuals or commercial concerns.

As in the past, Oxford will continue to provide conservation and restoration work for building specialists. Frequently, when working on the Sheldonian and other University buildings, Symm craftsmen will find themselves once again restoring the work of their forerunners from a previous generation. It is a continuous process, and as long as there is a public will to preserve, which seems likely with the growth of environmental consciousness, then companies like Symm will find ready outlets for their services. Confidence in the future, while tempered with the wisdom to acknowledge the ups and downs of the building industry, nevertheless prompted the Group in the mid 1990s to invest heavily in new technology and to extend significantly its Osney Mead base through the purchase of adjacent premises.

Drawing room, Rutland Gate, London, following refurbishment, 1996

Mahogany media cabinet for Manhattan apartment, New York, USA

Any responsible building company has to be concerned with the reputation of the industry as a whole and Symm is no exception. The 20th century has coined the term 'cowboy builders', although any Symm craftsman can testify to finding botched jobs from every period of history. Nevertheless, Symm like many others sees that the future prospects for the industry depend on it getting its house in order. The answer is to insist on quality, but this is something which is actually quite difficult to define. Everyone says, of course, that they apply the strictest standards of quality. However, the word is frequently misused, so that what is really meant is consistency. In other words, products will be manufactured to specification or staff trained to handle services in a certain pre determined manner, but neither may achieve the best possible result. There may be no unpleasant surprises, but on the other hand there is not likely to be much in the way of inspiration, innovation or excellence either. Unfortunately, over exposure of the term 'quality' has created a danger that people may become unsatisfied and cynical about something which, in its true sense, is highly desirable.

Symm has for some years been presenting clients with brief written guidelines entitled 'The Symm Approach'. These outline what the customer can expect from the company and its philosophy of service. The statements it makes are straightforward, revealing and presented as a list of 'some good reasons for choosing Symm Group', namely:

- A caring, sympathetic and helpful approach permeates all stages of the building process.
- Positive thinking and problem solving are key attitudes.
- Advice and guidance willingly given where sought, based on a wealth of experience over the whole spectrum of building activities (normally free of charge).
- Working relationships based on mutual trust a strong feature.
- Utmost respect for completion dates. Preplanning, programming and project management are focused on achieving, or beating, agreed targets.
- Avoidance of claim-consciousness; preferring to agree a sensible and fair price at the outset.
- Whilst not always cheapest, consistent value for money.
- Satisfied clients a prime objective.
- High proportion of repeat clients (Merton College, Oxford, a current client, first commissioned the firm as far back as the 1820s).
- Skills to develop a loosely defined idea from conception to completion, whether an entire building, purpose-made joinery, stonemasonry, building services or decorative finishes.
- General and specialist building, joinery, decoration, stonemasonry, mechanical and electrical services are all available 'in-house'; offering the full range of building services under single control.
- Apprentice-trained craftsmen teams embrace all skills required to execute traditional and contemporary high calibre work.
- Unique quality of joinery and woodwork.
- Skilled at working in occupied premises and alongside operational businesses with minimum disruption.
- Ideally suited to the difficult or demanding project, which may be beyond the capability of the average contractor.
- Historical work knowledge and expertise.
- Professionalism.
- Safety conscious, with comprehensive Safety Policy procedures and record.
- Symm has an unbroken record of fine building commissions, particularly in the Colleges of Oxford University, dating from 1815.

Finishing touches

Entrance Hall, Stretton Hall, Cheshire, 1995

Tusmore Park: new entrance gateway and lodges, 1996

- A dedicated tradition of service has been built up over almost 200 years; a strong foundation for the needs of today and demands of the future.

Taken together, these guideline statements provide a framework for handling any type of project, large or small. They work well in practice because everyone involved understands what they are about. In fact, they are the essence of what Symm has always aimed for, affecting not only what was done on a job but how it was done. In the case of the latter, people who have dealt with Symm employees on projects tend to use terms like 'old fashioned courtesy' when describing their treatment of clients. It is a sad reflection that courtesy should be thought of as 'old fashioned' at all, but since fashion is inclined to be cyclical, one can but hope for change in the future.

The coming years for the building industry are likely to be increasingly competitive, but this pressure will see the end of many of the inefficient and sometimes dishonest operators that give it a bad name. This partly relies on clients being more aware of the importance of professionalism and service.

The cheapest option may frequently turn out to be a bungled job because the builder hasn't thought it through or has skimped on labour and materials. In either case it will often turn out more expensive in the long run as well as creating endless bad feeling along the way. Confrontational attitudes between clients and their builders have been a feature of recent years, and Symm hopes that the litigation mentality that characterises so many building projects will be replaced in the future by the will to negotiate deals that are mutually fair. The Group's long standing relationships with Oxford's colleges supply examples of good practice which reflect well on both parties in the transactions. There is no arrogance or complacency intended in mentioning this, simply that rubbing along together for generations is bound to bring up some useful pointers for successful business relationships. Repeat business is always the best testimonial.

In a nutshell, the future for Symm is an optimistic one, so long as society continues to value its architectural heritage and to look for high standards in building, repair and refurbishment. The next 180 years will obviously see huge changes and Symm plans to be there to shape at least some of them in wood, natural stone and other traditional materials.

Oxford University Real Tennis Club: new club house and facilities, 1997

Symm House, Osney Mead, Oxford: Headquarters of the Symm Group since 1969

Appendix: CHRONOLOGICAL LIST OF BUILDINGS

YEAR	PROJECT	COST	ARCHITECT
1815-1846	**DANIEL EVANS**		
1815	Wesleyan Chapel, Bishop Street, Leicester.	£4,900	The Revd. W. Jenkins
1815-16	Wesleyan Chapel, Gold Street, Northampton.		The Revd. W. Jenkins
1816-17	Wesleyan Chapel, New Inn Hall Street, Oxford.	£2,965	The Revd. W. Jenkins
1820-22	Magdalen Hall (later Hertford College).	£10,450	E.W. Garbett
1820	Chiselhampton House: Portico, alterations, additions		D. EVANS
1822-26	Magdalen College: north and east ranges.	£20,484	J. Parkinson
1823	Merton College: Chapel altered.		
1824	Magdalen College: New Building wings added.		T. Harrison
1824	Nuneham Courtenay Rectory.		D. EVANS
1826	Radcliffe Asylum (now the Warneford Hospital).	£8,246	R. Ingleman
1826-27	Great Tew Church: alterations.	£1,245	T. Rickman
1828-29	Nos. 34-36 St. Giles', Oxford.		D. EVANS
1829	Pembroke College: front raised and remodelled, quad refaced.	£2,898	D. EVANS
1832	St. Aldate's Church, Oxford: restored.		H.J. Underwood
1832	Nos. 20-22 St. John Street, Oxford.		D. EVANS
1838	Pembroke College: East range refaced.	£5,270	D. EVANS
1839	Churcham Vicarage, Gloucestershire.		D. EVANS
1833-34	Exeter College: Broad Street range (east).	£3,574	H.J. Underwood
1841	Great Haseley Church: restored.		J.M. Derick
1845-46	Pembroke College: Chapel quad, north range.	£5,287	C. Hayward
1846-1874	**JOSHUA R. SYMM**		
1850	All Souls College: west front refaced.		
1854-56	Exeter College: Broad Street range (tower and west).	£3,976	G.Gilbert Scott
1855	Shotover House: wings added.		
1856-57	Exeter College: Library.		G.Gilbert Scott
1856-59	Exeter College: Chapel.	£11,591	G.Gilbert Scott
1857-58	Exeter College: Rector's Lodgings.		G.Gilbert Scott
1858	Exeter College: rooms south of Broad Street.		G.Gilbert Scott
1859-62	University College: Library.	£5,141	G.Gilbert Scott
1860	University College: Buttery.	£500	G.Gilbert Scott
1862-63	University College: Chapel altered.	£2,754	G.Gilbert Scott
1862-65	Christ Church: Meadow Buildings.	£22,000	T.N. Deane
1863	Union Society: Reading and Writing Rooms.		W. Wilkinson
1863-64	Ashmolean Museum (Old): alterations.	£1,533	C. Buckeridge

YEAR	PROJECT	COST	ARCHITECT
1867	23, Banbury Road, Oxford, for Revd. S. J. Holmes. (now Felstead House)		E.G. Bruton
1868-70	Clarendon Laboratory.	£10,282	T.N. Deane
1870-71	Nos. 133, 135, 137 & 139 Woodstock Road, Oxford.		
1870-76	Christ Church Cathedral, Oxford: restoration.	£24,000	G.Gilbert Scott
1871	St. Ebbe's Infant School, Paradise Square, Oxford.		B. Champneys
1871-78	Wesley Memorial Church, Oxford.	£13,999	C. Bell
1871-83	University Church of St. Mary, Oxford: restoration		
	St. Giles' Church, Oxford.		
	Church of St. Mary and St. John, Cowley Road, Oxford.		
1873	64 Banbury Road, Oxford.		E.G. Bruton
1873-75	Observatory.	£4,668	C. Barry Junior
1873-74	St. Aldate's Church, Oxford: Tower rebuilt.		J.T. Christopher
1873-76	St. Edward's School, Oxford: Chapel.	£5,000	W. Wilkinson

1874-1887   J.R. SYMM & Co.

YEAR	PROJECT	COST	ARCHITECT
1874	New College Choir School.		Field and Castle
1874-80	Christ Church: restoration of Tom Quad.		
1875	St. Frideswide's Vicarage, 19 Botley Road, Oxford.		H.G.W. Drinkwater
1874-80	Christ Church: refacing of Tom Quad, Fell Tower, Chapter House.		
	Wolsey Tower built.		Bodley & Garner
1876-84	Bodleian Library: restored.	£26,440	T.G. Jackson
1877	Radcliffe Camera: restored.		A. Waterhouse
1877	All Souls College, Chapel: stone panelling.		
1877	New College: Inner quad parapet rebuilt.		
1877-78	Observatory: lecture room and library.	£2,145	C. Barry
1877-79	Inorganic Chemistry Laboratory.	£8,268	T.N. Deane
1877-79	University College: conversion of existing Master's Lodgings into student rooms		
1878-81	Bodleian Library: repairs.		T.G. Jackson
1878	31-32 Queen Street, Oxford: Hyde Outfitters.		F. Codd
1878-80	Post Office, St. Aldate's, Oxford.	£10,000	E.G. Rivers
1879	Oxford High School for Girls		T.G. Jackson
1879	St. Edward's School: Gatehouse.		W. Wilkinson
1879	Blenheim Palace: West front stonework.		
1879	No. 8 Kingston Road, Oxford.		T. AXTELL
1879-80	Woodperry House: wings added.	£4,500	F. Codd
1880	Old Methodist Chapel, Oxford: converted for Sunday School.		
1880	St. John's College: New Quad.		
1880s	University College: repairing and refacing stonework.		
1881	Christ Church: drainage system.		

YEAR	PROJECT	COST	ARCHITECT
1881	Wycliffe Hall: south wing, with Library and 11 sets of rooms.		Wilkinson & Moore
1882	Baker furniture warehouse, Broad Street, Oxford.		F. Codd
1882-84	Indian Institute: north half.		B. Champneys
1882-82	Brasenose College: south quad, west and north sides.		T.G. Jackson
1882-83	St. John's Hospital, Cowley St. John, Oxford: extensions.		J.L. Pearson
1883	No. 14 Queen Street, Oxford.		
1883	Christ Church: 3 lecture rooms, stone walls of Hall restored.		
1884	Nos. 137, 139 Woodstock Road, Oxford.		
1884-85	Physiology Laboratory.	£6,000	T.N. Deane & Son
1885	Keble College: Laboratory.		
1885-86	Clarendon Press: Machine room.		
1885-86	Pitt Rivers Museum.		T.N. Deane & Son
1886	Trinity College: Kettle Hall, lecture room.		
1886-88	Merton College: Chapel restored.		T.G. Jackson
1886-94	Somerville College: West Building i.		H.W. Moore
1887-1926	**SYMM & Co.**		
1887	Queen's College: part West range.		
1887-88	Hertford College: Gate and hall.		T.G. Jackson
1888	No. 15, Norham Gardens, Oxford: Large new wing		Tollit
1888	All Saints' Church: Tower and south front restoration		
1888	14 Fyfield Road, Oxford (Fyfield Lodge).		
1888-92	Radcliffe Infirmary: alterations.		
1889	Ashmolean Museum: Beaumont Street block.		H.W. Moore
1889-91	Cowley St. John Hospital: new buildings.		
1889	No. 26-27 Broad Street, Oxford.		C.C. Rolfe
1889	Lincoln College: Hall restored and roof revealed.		T.G. Jackson
1890	St. Matthew's Church, Grandpont, Oxford.	£6,520	Christopher & White
1890	Cornbury Park: stonework refaced.		
1890s	Wolvercote Paper Mill		
1891	Botanic Garden: arch releaded and stonework.		T.G. Jackson
1891	Merton College: hall turret, chapel heating.		
1891	St. Barnabas' Girls School, Oxford: extension.		
1892	St. Barnabas' Church, Jericho, Oxford: enlarged and repaired.		
1892	Parish Institute, Jericho, Oxford.		
1892	Merton College: Bell turret restored.		T.G. Jackson
1892-93	Department of Human Anatomy.		H.W. Moore
1892-94	St. Aldate's Church of England School.		
1892-96	Church of St. Mary, Oxford: restored.	£11,633	T.G. Jackson

YEAR	PROJECT	COST	ARCHITECT
1893	Christ Church: Choir School.		H.W. Moore
1893-95	Somerville College: West Building ii.		H.W. Moore
1893-94	Ashmolean Museum: rear galleries.	£1,500	H.W. Moore
1895-96	All Saints' Church: renovated as City Church.		T.G. Jackson
1896	Acland Hospital, Oxford.		T.G. Jackson
1896	Wycliffe Hall, 52-54 Banbury Road, Oxford: Chapel		W. Wallace
1897	61a Banbury Road, Oxford.		
1897	Carfax Tower: new stair turret and parapets.		T.G. Jackson
1898	Residence, Mansfield Road, Oxford. (now School of Geography)		B. Jackson
1898-1901	Morphological Laboratory.		J.J. Stevens & H. Root
1900	Wadham College: repairs in Chapel and Hall.		
1901	Pathology Laboratory.	£10,000	J.A. Soulter
1902	Bodleian: heating flue moved.		
1903	University College: Front Quad and High Street frontage restored.		
1904-06	Christ Church: alterations.		
1905	University College: Logic Lane bridge.		
1905	St. John's College: Canterbury Quad columns replaced.		
1905	No. 12, Charlbury Road, Oxford.		J.R. SYMM
1905	No. 14, Charlbury Road, Oxford.		J.R. SYMM
1905	No. 16, Charlbury Road, Oxford.		N.G. Harrison
1906	Sheldonian Theatre: staircase improvements.	£23,170	Smith & Brewer
1906	Old Ashmolean.		T.G. Jackson
1906-07	Merton College: St. Alban Hall quad.		
1906-07	All Saints' Church: NWE sides refaced; railings to E.		
1907	University College: extending 17th century Hall and opening up roof.		
1907	Geology Department: extra floor.		
1907	No. 10, Charlbury Road, Oxford.		N.G. Harrison
1907-09	Clarendon Building: stonework.		J.R. Wilkins
1908	Worcester College: Chapel and Hall cornice rebuilt.		
1908	Nos. 14, 16, Moreton Road, Oxford.		
1908-09	Christ Church: St. Aldate's front & Tom Tower restoration		W.D. Caröe
1908-09	Christ Church: baths in Tom & Peckwater Quads, Meadow Buildings.		
1909	Queen's College: Cupola upper part rebuilt in Portland stone.		
1909	Worcester College: Provost's Lodgings, redecorate Hall and Library.		
1910	Queen's College: Clock tower renovation.		
1910	No. 22, Charlbury Road, Oxford.		N.W. Harrison

YEAR	PROJECT	COST	ARCHITECT
1911	Christ Church: Kitchen alterations.	£4,450	W.D. Caröe
1912	No. 24, Charlbury Road, Oxford.		
1914	University College: upper floors of 90 High Street converted to student use.		
1920	Queen's College: staircase alterations.		
1922	No. 26, Charlbury Road, Oxford.		
1923	Bodleian Library: new oak floor in Binder's room, repairing/replacing fine woodwork throughout the building.		
1923-27	All Souls College: stone restoration to twin towers		E.P. Warren FSA
1924	Nos. 32 & 34 Victoria Road, Oxford.		

SYMM & Co. Ltd. 1926

YEAR	PROJECT	COST	ARCHITECT
1924-30	Christ Church: Peckwater Quad, full stone restoration		
1926-27	St. Edmund Hall: extension of Undergraduate Library.		H.S. Rogers
1927	Old Ashmolean, Oxford: improvements.		
1927	Hernes House, Children's Home.		
1930s-90s	Blenheim Palace: on-going major stone restoration projects. (APS Masonry)		Thomas Rayson Ptnrs.
1931	Pembroke College: alterations		
1933	Christ Church: 2, Brewer Street, alterations.		
1934	St. Edmund Hall: Canterbury Building.		R. Feilding Dodd
1947	St. Mary the Virgin: Chancel roof. Reinstatement following fire damage.		
1949-50	Oriel College, Wyatt Building, Senior Library: restoration and new copper roof following fire damage.		
1954	St. Hilda's College: new Principal's Lodgings.		Sir Albert Richardson RA
1958	Merton College: Library alterations, re-arrangement and oak furniture		S.E. Dykes Bower
1959	Queen's College: new Provost's Lodgings.		Raymond Erith
1960-80s	Christ Church: restored external fabric and improvements to: Great Quadrangle, Great Hall, Cathedral, St. Aldate's Front, Tom Tower, Kitchens, Old Library, Law Library, Priory House, Deanery, Peckwater Quad, Killcanon, Chapter House, Wolsey Tower (a century after it had been built by J.R. Symm).		The Playne Vallance Partnership
1961	St. Aldate's Church: extension		J.M. Surman
1962	Worcester College: Provost's Lodgings. Major refurbishment/alteration.		Carden & Godfrey
1962-63	Merton College: new Warden's Lodgings.		Carden & Godfrey
1963-65	Westminster Bank Ltd., High Street, Oxford: major improvements and Alfred Street extensions.		Norman Bailey Samuels & Partners
1970	Heythrop Park, Oxon: major refurbishment/alteration.	£750,000	B. Worrall
1970s-80s	Ditchley Park, Oxon: refurbishment, restoration, alteration and decoration		Gray Baynes & Shew
1973	Wantage Civic Hall		Astam Design Ptnrs.
1975	Ferry Pool and Leisure Centre, North Oxford.		F. Jewell

YEAR	PROJECT	COST	ARCHITECT
1983	Residence, Virginia, USA: Oak panelled Library.	£175,000	D. Easton
1984	Residence, Virginia, USA: Chapel interior	£117,000	D. Easton
1984	Le Manoir aux Quat' Saisons, Great Milton: phase I	£450,000	D. Bradley
1985	Thame Park, Oxfordshire: major refurbishment and restoration.	£3m	Peter Luck & Ptnrs.
1985-86	Palace of Westminster, Riverside Terrace: major stone restoration. (APS Masonry)		
1986	River House, Manhattan, New York, USA: interior woodwork.	£130,000	R. Couturier
1988	Champneys Health Resort: major improvements, alteration and refurbishment.	£1m	Blissett MacDonald Associates
1988	Residence, Fort Worth, Texas, USA: Study interior woodwork.	£95,000	J. Dixon III
1988-92	Taplow Court, Buckinghamshire.	£6 m. +	P. Johnson
1989	Oxford University Sports Ground: Rugby Fives Courts	£100,000	Surveyor to the Univ.
1990	Le Manoir aux Quat' Saisons, Great Milton: phase II	£1.8m	D. Bradley
1992	Uppark, Sussex: window renewals and painting following fire damage.	£220,000	The Conservation Practice
1992	Grace Episcopal Church, New Bedford, MA, USA: carved oak interior woodwork and stone altar following fire damage.	£100,000	Wise Surma Jones Architects
1992-97	All Souls College: upgrading, alterations and refurbishment projects, including Warden's Lodgings (4 phases)	£1.5m	N. Machin
1993	Rathmoyle House, Northern Ireland: alterations/refurbishment.		M. Priest
1994	New College: alterations to Wyatt Library.	£350,000	Rodney Melville & Ptnrs.
1994-96	Residence, Winnington Road, Hampstead, London: major extension, upgrade and redecoration.	£5.8m	Gilmore Hankey Kirke
1995	Iffley Church, Oxford: internal refurbishment.	£110,000	Caröe and Partners
1995	Sheldonian Theatre, Oxford: restoration and repairs to Cupola.	£60,000	Surveyor to the Univ.
1995	Stretton Hall, Cheshire: refurbishment/restoration/redecoration.	£1.4m	M. Priest
1995	Lincoln College Chapel: internal refurbishments.	£84,000	The Sarum Ptnrship.
1996	Residence, Rutland Gate, London: extension/refurbishment.	£900,000	M. Priest
1996	Woodperry, Oxfordshire: major refurbishment/restoration.	£1.5m	Hall & Ensom - Surveyors.
1996	Residence, Fort Worth, Texas, USA: Library interior woodwork	£110,000	J. Dixon III
1996	Residence, Richmond, London: refurbishment and creation of penthouse suite.	£650,000	T. Hatton
1997	University College: Master's Lodgings refurbishment	£150,000	
1997-98	Le Manoir aux Quat' Saisons, Great Milton: phase III	£5m	PDA Limited
1998	Lincoln College: major refurbishment and restoration		N. Machin
1998	Hyde Park Gate, London: major refurbishment		Moren Greenhalgh

NOTE ON THE VALUE OF MONEY

Most of the money values expressed in this book - wealth, incomes, profits, asset values etc. - relate to the early, middle or late nineteenth century. Throughout this period and indeed up to the first world war, the purchasing power of money was comparatively stable; if anything prices tended to fall. The first world war brought a sharp rise in prices but the inter-war years saw prices falling again. Inflation returned in the second world war and has continued at a variable rate ever since, quickening especially in the 1970s.

As a general guide, a multiple of sixty converts nineteenth century values to those of the present day. Thus a weekly wage of 15 shillings, typical in Oxford in the late 19th century would be about £45 today; a modest tradesman's fortune of £10,000 in the same period would be the equivalent of £600,000 in today's money. Similarly a building contract costed at £20,000 would correspond to £1.2m.

ACKNOWLEDGEMENTS

With thanks to the following for their invaluable assistance in the research and preparation for this History:

The Archivists and Librarians of the Colleges of the University of Oxford
Mr. Geoffrey Beard, RIBA
Mr. John Besley
The Bodleian Library
Mr. Roger Bonnett
Mrs. Elizabeth Boardman
Sir Howard Colvin
The Revd. John Cowdrey
Mrs. A.J Croft - The Late A.J. Croft's, *Oxford's Clarendon Laboratory* (unpublished)
The Guildhall Library
Mr. Ronnie Gunn
Mr. Jim Levi
Mr Paul Lucas
Miss Yvonne Macken
Oxford County Record Office
The Public Record Office
The Revd. John Reynolds
Dr. John Sanders - Archivist, The Clarendon Laboratory
Miss Alexandra Scott-Malden
Mrs. Anne Sharpe
Mrs. Ann Spokes Symonds
Mrs. Elspeth Villet

PICTURE ACKNOWLEDGEMENTS

Numbers refer to the page where illustration appears. (Number in brackets is the archive reference):

Adkin: 109, 117
Ashmolean Museum, University of Oxford (all Almanack pictures): 12 (E748ci), 16 (O1926). 20 (E926), 31 (E748 ii), 35 (E748 14), 49 (O1864), 51 (O1881), 53 (O1862), 72 (O1892), 81 (E927)
Barker Evans Photographic Design, Oxford: Jacket illustration
Bodleian Library, Oxford: 36 (Gt. Tew), 43, 44, 47, 48, 78 (minn coll.1/39), 92 (minn 30/3/27)
Barry Capper: 57, 89
Simon Chapman, Oxon: 97
By kind permission of the Governing Body of Christ Church, Oxford: 16, 51, 52, 82
Clarendon Laboratory: 55, 56
Country Life: 120
John Cowan: 106
The Rector and Fellows of Exeter College, Oxford: 15, 42, 48
Gillman and Soame, Oxford: 29
Graham Photography: 111
HMSO, © Crown Copyright: 19
Ivor Fields: 99
James Kerr: 123
Leicestershire Museum, Arts and Records Service: 29
Le Manoir aux Quat' Saisons: 113
Di Lewis: 122
The President and Fellows of Magdalen College, Oxford: 8, 32, 33
The Warden and Fellows of Merton College, Oxford: 105
The Provost and Fellows of Oriel College, Oxford: 104
Christine Ottewell: 115
Oxfordshire County Council, Department of Leisure and Arts: 14, 18, 31, 36, 37, 40, 53, 56, 61, 63, 64, 67, 69, 72, 73, 77, 83, 85
Oxfordshire Health Archives: 34
Pitt Rivers Museum, Oxford: 66
© The Post Office, 1936 by kind permission: 67
Rover Group: 119
The Principal and Fellows of St. Edmund Hall, Oxford: 91
St. Edward's School, Oxford: 58, 59
The President and Fellows of St. John's College, Oxford: 83
Symm Group Archives: 10, 22, 24, 25, 29, 30, 35, 49, 70, 74, 76, 80, 85, 86, 88, 82, 83, 99, 106, 109, 117, 122, 123
Thomas Photos, Oxford: Frontispiece, 37, 38, 39, 45, 46, 50, 52, 60, 65, 75, 79, 84, 87, 89, 94, 95, 96, 98, 99, 100, 101, 102, 103, 104, 105, 106, 107, 108, 110, 112, 114, 116, 117, 118, 120, 121, 124, 125
Master and Fellows of University College, Oxford: 79, 83

INDEX

Page numbers in italics refer to the illustrations

Acland Hospital 74, 129
All Saints' Church 73, *74*, 128, 129
All Souls College 53, *89*, 126, 127, 130, 131
Ashmolean Museum 54, 126, 128, 129
Axtell, Alfred 81
Axtell and Perry 105
Axtell, Dudley R. 89, 91, 92
Axtell, Graham J. 89, 92, 94, *99*
Axtell, Malcolm J. 4, 92
Axtell Perry Symm Masonry (APS Masonry)
    105, 110, 115, 118
Axtell, Peter G. 92
Axtell, Richard J. 85, 89, 91, 92
Axtell, Thomas J. *59*, 60, 70, 78, 80, 92, 127
Axtell, William 105

Barry, Charles 13, 41, 127
Benfield and Loxley 85
Blenheim Palace *108*, 119, 127, 130
Bodleian Library 16, 22, *31*, *60*, 62, *63*, 64,
    65, 74, *86*, 89, 91, *92*, 127, 129, 130,
    139
Bodley and Garner 51
Brasenose College 66, 73, 128
Bruton, E.G. 56, 74, 127
Buckler, John 11, 54
Butterfield, W. 23, 53, 54

Caröe, W.D. 81, 129, 130, 131
Champneys, Basil 51, 65, 67, 84, 127, 128
Chequers 119
Chiselhampton House *35*, 126
Christ Church 13, 14, 15, *16*, *21*, 43, 47,
    49, *51*, *52*, 53, 60, 68, *69*, *81*, *83*, 86,
    89, *97*, *98*, *99*, 105, *106*, 127, 128, 129,
    130, 139
Clarendon Laboratory 54, *55*, *56*, 127

Deane and Woodward 15
Deane, T.N. 49, 54, 65, 126, 127, 139
Dodgson, The Revd. Charles (Lewis Carroll)
    49, 52

Evans, Daniel 7, *9*, 9–13, 14, 23, 27, *29*,
    29–41, *31*, *34*, *35*, *36*, *38*, *40*, 43, 60,
    72, 126

Evans, Richard 60, 79–80, 85
Exeter College 10, 13, *14*, *15*, *38*, *43*, *44*,
    47, *48*, 49, 53, 71, 85, 86, 101, 126, 139

Fowler, John 105, *106*
Franklin of Deddington 54, 85

Garbett, William 9, 10, 13, 30, 126

Hart, Benjamin 62, 70, 73, 79, 80
Hart, Harry J. 79, 89, 91
Hart, Leonard 89, 92
Hayward, Charles 13
Hertford College 9, 10, 30, 31, *72*, 126, 128
    Magdalen Hall *9*, *10*, 11, 30, *31*
Heythrop Park *109*, 110, 130
Howard, Thomas 16, 62
Howse, H.E. 92
Howse, Tom 79

Indian Institute *64*, 65, 128
Inorganic Chemistry Laboratory *65*, 127

Jackson, T.G. 51, 63, 65, 66, 74, 77, 79,
    80, 85, 127, 128, 129, 139
Jenkins, The Revd. William 29, 126
Jesus College 54

Keble College 54, 128
Kingerlee 68, 77, 85
Knowles 25, 66

Lady Margaret Hall 85
Le Manoir aux Quat' Saisons *113*, 131
Liddell, Henry 13, 15, 49
Lincoln College *74*, 128, 131

Magdalen College 9, 10, 11, 30, 31, *32*,
    33, 77, 105, *106*, 126
Magdalen Hall
    see Hertford College
Merton College *35*, *60*, 84, 86, 89, *95*, *103*,
    105, *114*, 126, 128, 129, 130
Moore, H.W. 65, 74, 79, *83*, 128, 129

New College 54, 71, 127, 131
Nuneham Courtenay Rectory *36*, 126

Oriel College 103, *104*, 130

Palace of Westminster 13, 110, *111*, 119, 131
Parkinson, Joseph 11, 13, 31, 126
Parnell of Rugby 25, 54, 65, 77, 85
Pembroke College *12*, 13, *37*, *40*, 41, 97,
    126, 130
Pitt Rivers Museum 65, *66*, 74, 128
Post Office *67*, 127

Queen's College 83, *84*, 101, *103*, 128,
    129, 130

Radcliffe Camera *31*, 86, *89*, 127
Radcliffe Infirmary 74, 77, 128
Radcliffe Science Library 77
Radley College 74

Scott, Gilbert George *13, 14,* 15, 16, 23, 43,
    44, 47, 49, 51, 53, 54, 67, 126, 139
Sharp and Howse 79, 115, 118, *119*
Sheldonian Theatre 65, *80*, *120*, 129, 131,
    139
Somerville College 128, 129
St. Aldate's Church 37, 56, 126, 127, 128,
    130
St. Catherine's College 13
St. Edmund Hall *91*, 130
St. Edward's School *59*, 127
St. Giles' 11, *38*, 41, 70, 80, 126
St. Hilda's College *103*, 130
St. John Street 12

St. John's College 12, *83*, 127, 129
St. Mary the Virgin 74, *77*, 130
Symm and Co 16–17, 60, 68–70
    Financial Results 78–80, 91
    First Partnership 62, 70–71
    Second Partnership 73–89
    Working Practices 68–70, 85–86
Symm, Joshua R. 13–16, 27, 38, 41, 43,
    43–71, *44, 54,* 68, 73, 78, 86, 97, 126,
    129

Taplow Court 111, *112*, 131
Thame Park *110*, 131
Trinity College *105*, 128

Underwood, H.J. 14, 37, 38, 56, 126
University College 15, 43, *53, 54, 66, 79,
    83, 94, 100*, 126, 127, 129, 130, 131
Uppark 119, *120*, 131

Wadham College *118*, 129
Warneford Hospital
    Radcliffe Asylum *34*, 126
Waterhouse, A. 23, 53, 127
Wesleyan Chapels
    Leicester *29*, 126
    Northampton 126
    Oxford 9, *30*, 70, 126
Woodperry House *68*, 127, 131
Worcester College 85, *101, 103*, 129, 130
Wyatt, Margaret 24
Wycliffe Hall 66, 128, 129